Managing Your Drug
or Alcohol Problem

Therapist Guide

Dennis C. Daley
G. Alan Marlatt

From The Psychological Corporation

Printed in the United States of America
    3 4 5 6 7 8 9 10 11 12 A B C D E
0158131673

Table of Contents

▪ Part 4: Relapse Prevention and Progress Measurement 113

Tables

Series Introduction

The psychosocial treatment program in this Therapist Guide is part of a series of empirically supported treatment programs. The purpose of the series is to disseminate knowledge about specific interventions for which systematic research studies indicate effectiveness. This treatment program, along with others in the series, has been clearly demonstrated to have empirical support for its efficacy in treating the particular condition you are addressing. However, clinicians operate with a wide variety of clients with different characteristics who are treated in different types of settings. Thus, the manner in which the treatment program is implemented will be the decision of the treating clinician with his or her unparalleled knowledge of the local clinical situation and the particular patient under care. Although some data indicate that allegiance to the treatment protocol produces the best results in a variety of clinical settings, only the treating clinician is in a position to judge the degree of flexibility required to achieve optimal results.

We sincerely hope that you find the psychosocial treatment program, of which this Therapist Guide forms an integral part, useful in your clinical practice. This Therapist Guide is meant to accompany various clinical materials that you would be prescribing for clients in the implementation of this program. This Therapist Guide is designed to assist clinicians in the systematic administration of the particular treatment program being implemented. As such it will highlight relevant information and exercises to which the clinician will want to attend in sessions. The guide also presents typical problems that may arise in the implementation of specific therapeutic procedures and suggests means for solving these problems. Thus, therapists may want to review the brief individual chapters corresponding to each therapeutic session or intervention prior to conducting sessions, perhaps while reviewing case notes.

Although the Therapist Guide is not a full description of the theoretical approach and empirical work that supports this treatment, references for additional information are provided. We encourage review of these readings for a comprehensive understanding. Please let us know if you have suggestions for improving our systems for helping you deliver effective psychosocial treatments for clients under your care.

David H. Barlow

Boston, Massachusetts

Acknowledgments

We wish to thank Judith Gordon, PhD, and Natalie Daley, MSW, for their helpful critiques of this Therapist Guide. We also wish to thank David Barlow, PhD, for his interest in this project. Special thanks to Cindy Hurney for her creative design of this guide and for all the other tasks she completed on this Therapist Guide and the accompanying Client Workbook.

Finally, we wish to acknowledge the efforts and contributions made by various individuals at The Psychological Corporation, especially John Dilworth, President; Joanne Lenke, PhD, Executive Vice President; and Aurelio Prifitera, PhD, Vice President and Director of the Psychological Measurement Group. As Project Director, Tom Cayton, PhD, has contributed to the high quality of the Therapist Guide. Special appreciation is also extended to those persons whose diligent and meticulous efforts were essential in preparing the Therapist Guide. Among these individuals are Mark Morris, MA, Research Analyst; Stephanie Tong, MA, Research Assistant; Kathy Overstreet, Supervising Editor; Jennifer Knoblock, Consulting Editor; Hope Doty, Editor; and Javier Flores, Designer.

About the Authors

Dennis C. Daley is director of the Center for Psychiatric and Chemical Dependency Services and an assistant professor of psychiatry at the University of Pittsburgh Medical Center, Department of Psychiatry, and at Western Psychiatric Institute and Clinic in Pittsburgh. Mr. Daley has been involved in managing and providing treatment services for alcohol and drug problems for nearly two decades. He has published many family and client educational books, workbooks, and videotapes on recovery from alcohol and drug problems, recovery from psychiatric disorders, recovery from dual disorders, and relapse prevention. Mr. Daley teaches on these subjects throughout the United States and other countries. He is also involved in several federally funded research projects on treatment of cocaine addiction and the treatment of dual disorders. Mr. Daley authored the highly successful *Living Sober Interactive Videotape Series* and the *Promise of Recovery Educational Videotape Series*.

G. Alan Marlatt, PhD, is director of the Addictive Behaviors Research Center and Professor of Psychology at the University of Washington in Seattle. Dr. Marlatt has been involved in research and treatment of addictive disorders for nearly three decades. He has written many books and articles related to assessment and treatment of alcohol and drug problems, relapse prevention, and harm reduction. He wrote the first major book on relapse prevention. Dr. Marlatt has received many research grants and is currently supported by a Research Scientist Award from the National Institute of Alcohol Abuse and Alcoholism. He teaches and consults worldwide on many subjects related to prevention, assessment, and treatment of alcohol and drug problems. In 1990, Dr. Marlatt received the Jellinek Memorial Award for outstanding contributions to knowledge in the field of alcohol studies. He has made outstanding scientific, clinical, and educational contributions to the field of substance abuse.

Part 1

Overview of Substance Use Problems and Assessment

Chapter 1

Introduction and Plan
for the Therapist Guide

Introduction and Overview

This Therapist Guide reviews practical issues in the assessment
and treatment of all types of substance use disorders. It is designed
to accompany the *Managing Your Drug or Alcohol Problem Client
Workbook*. The information and recovery strategies can be used with
clients who abuse or are dependent on alcohol, sedatives, tobacco,
cocaine, methamphetamines and other stimulants, heroin and other
opioids, cannabis, hallucinogens, and inhalants. The guide provides
clinicians with strategies for working with substance use disorders
by focusing on specific issues involved in both stopping substance
abuse and changing behaviors or lifestyle aspects that contribute
to continued substance abuse. The information presented in this guide
and in the accompanying Client Workbook is derived from several
sources: empirical, clinical, and self-help literature, as well as the authors'
many years of experience developing treatment programs and providing
direct treatment services.

There are many different types of substance use problems in terms
of severity and adverse effects on the client and family. Therefore,
treatment will be more effective if the recovery approach is tailored
to the needs and problems of the specific client. It is important to note
that no single recovery program fits all clients. A challenge for clinicians
is to adapt treatment strategies to the specific problems and issues
of a particular client.

This guide discusses professional approaches and attitudes toward
individuals who abuse substances, assessment, psychosocial
and pharmacotherapeutic treatment of substance abuse, and self-help

programs. It provides an overview of the recovery and relapse processes. The major thrust of this guide is to provide practical clinical strategies to address the most common issues associated with substance use disorders, including

- engaging clients in treatment,
- managing cravings and thoughts of using,
- resisting social pressures to use,
- dealing with family and interpersonal conflicts,
- building a recovery support system,
- dealing with emotions,
- achieving balanced living,
- identifying and managing relapse warning signs and high-risk factors,
- interrupting and learning from a lapse or relapse, and
- measuring progress.

Intended Audience

The first six chapters of this guide provide a brief and basic overview of causes, symptoms, effects, assessment, psychosocial treatments, and pharmaceutical treatments of substance use disorders. Experienced therapists who are familiar with this information can skip these chapters and focus on Chapters 7–19, which describe the common clinical themes and interventions in treatment sessions. Less experienced therapists or those who do not work primarily with substance use disorders will find that the first six chapters provide a general introduction to understanding substance use disorders.

The treatment strategies discussed in Chapters 7–19 can easily be used with clients, regardless of the therapist's theoretical or clinical orientation. For example, the chapters on managing cravings, managing thoughts of using substances, and dealing with emotions can be used by the 12-step oriented counselor as well as by therapists who use more of a behavioral or cognitive approach to substance abuse treatment.

Chapters 7–19 can be used by any professional who is working with a client with a substance use problem. Each chapter can be used in one or more treatment sessions. The clinical interventions described in these chapters are all designed to engage the client actively in completing recovery assignments aimed at increasing personal awareness or facilitating positive change.

This guide can be used in brief treatment with the client and therapist as they jointly identify specific change issues to review and address during each session. It can also be used in a longer course of treatment, with the focus of the sessions shifting according to the needs and interests of the client. If a small, limited number of treatment sessions are used, they should be spread out over time so that the client has time to implement and modify change strategies learned in the sessions.

Therapists can review Chapters 7–19 in sequence for those clients who are in treatment for the first time, as they represent the most common issues faced in changing a substance use problem. Less psychologically threatening material is introduced in the early sessions. For clients who have recently relapsed, the therapist can decide with the client which chapters to review and in what order, based on the specific problems and issues presented by the client. Hence, the guide can be used flexibly, depending on where a particular client is in the change process. The clinical issues reviewed in this guide, such as dealing with emotions, can be revisited by clients as their treatment progresses.

How to Use the Client Workbook

This Therapist Guide provides a brief summary of issues discussed in the accompanying Client Workbook for the *Managing Your Drug or Alcohol Problem* program. The Client Workbook provides information on a variety of important substance use and recovery topics and offers interactive recovery assignments aimed at helping the client relate to the material in a personal way. This information can be used to identify target areas of change in the therapy or counseling process. The therapist can then help the client develop the requisite coping skills to facilitate personal or lifestyle changes. The specific issues addressed in the workbook can be adapted for clients in various stages of the change process. For example, clients in early recovery can focus on identifying harmful consequences of substance use and raising their level of motivation to change. Clients in later recovery can focus more attention on relapse prevention.

Clients in individual treatment can be assigned specific sections of the workbook to work on between treatment sessions. Treatment sessions can be used to explore each section in greater detail. The client's unique approach to recovery assignments and actual answers often provides rich material for treatment sessions.

Any of the workbook chapters that address recovery issues and strategies (Chapters 7–19) can easily be adapted for use in psychoeducational groups in residential, partial hospital, intensive outpatient, outpatient, or aftercare treatment settings. The recommended format for group treatment conducted in residential settings is as follows:

- Introduce the topic of the session and state why it is an important issue to consider in ongoing recovery.

- Select major points for discussion with group members.

- Instruct the participants on how to complete the worksheets.

- Use participants' answers to elaborate on specific recovery issues and coping strategies.

- If time permits, use behavioral rehearsals to illustrate how to deal with interpersonal issues such as refusing offers to use substances or dealing with family conflict.

Group sessions conducted in partial hospital, outpatient, or aftercare settings can use this format with a "check-in" period of 10 to 20 minutes preceding the discussion, in which participants report their last day of substance use and briefly discuss strong cravings, close calls, or actual lapses or relapses. Sessions can end with a "check-out" period, in which each client briefly states his or her plan for continued recovery. A major challenge for clinicians conducting topic-oriented recovery groups is to keep the group on the topic and get the clients to personally relate to the issues discussed to make the discussion more meaningful for them. Another challenge is to prevent one or two members from dominating the discussions or using the group solely to discuss their personal problems. Because psychoeducational groups aim to provide information and help participants develop coping skills, the group facilitator should ensure that the group holds to the topic unless the circumstances dictate otherwise. The group leader also needs to balance the discussion between problems or recovery challenges and coping strategies. Otherwise, groups will spend all or most of the time talking about problems and struggles, leaving little time to discuss what they can do to cope with these.

Structured psychoeducational group sessions can vary in length from 1 to 2 hours. In outpatient and aftercare settings, additional time is needed to provide clients an opportunity to report on their progress and plans for ongoing recovery. Small groups of 6 to 12 clients provide a better opportunity for interaction among group members and personal discussion of recovery issues. The specific topics of the group sessions can also easily be adapted as lectures for large groups of clients. The main limitations of lectures to large groups of clients are little, if any, opportunity to make the group an interactive experience and lack of adequate time for participants to complete the written exercises in which they personally relate to the material.

The Client Workbook is structured to present engagement and early recovery issues before middle and late recovery and maintenance issues. However, because recovery is not a linear process, the therapist can explore whichever issues are relevant to a client at a particular time. Also, many early recovery issues may be revisited later in treatment. For example, a client with 9 months of recovery may suddenly experience a significant increase in cravings for alcohol that are intense and worrisome, or new pressures to use drugs that lead to increased thoughts of using. The therapist would need to bring these issues to the front of the treatment agenda to reduce the likelihood of relapse.

Need for Additional Psychotherapy or Other Services

Many clients with substance use disorders have other psychiatric, psychological, interpersonal, or vocational problems that require psychotherapy or other types of specialized counseling. These include, but are not limited to, mood disorders, anxiety disorders, significant personality problems, serious marital and family problems, serious interpersonal deficits, lack of vocational skills, inability to find or keep a job, or other life problems. In many instances, once the client establishes a reasonable degree of stability regarding the substance use disorder, he or she is more ready to focus on other types of problems.

Therapists or counselors trained in psychotherapy can integrate additional interventions into their work with clients to address other difficulties. However, therapists or counselors who are comfortable focusing solely on substance use disorders will need a network of professionals to whom they can refer the client for help with other types of serious problems. In such cases, collaboration is needed to ensure that all professionals involved are working in an integrated fashion.

Other services, such as vocational assessment and counseling, may be needed to help in the client's long-term recovery. Therapists and counselors should also be able to facilitate the client's use of vocational resources as needed. They must use caution to avoid premature referral for vocational training for clients who have more severe types of substance use disorders and are unable to establish continuous and stable recovery. The client without stable recovery who is referred for vocational training is at risk for early dropout, leading to another "failure" experience. Additionally, this leads to poor use of limited funds available for vocational services.

Essential Skills for the Therapist

Effective clinical work with substance use problems requires versatility and flexibility. Content knowledge and clinical skills in the following areas are needed for the therapist to be effective with clients who have substance use disorders:

- assessing substance use, effects on the client, coping strategies, and relapse potential,

- developing a therapeutic alliance,

- enhancing motivation to examine substance use and to change,

- providing direct treatment by addressing specific recovery issues and problems,

- monitoring change in substance use patterns and related behaviors; measuring progress or lack of progress,

- collaborating with other service providers,

- referring for other needed services (e.g., medical, vocational, psychological, housing, economic, rehabilitation),

- providing linkage to self-help programs and other treatment programs, and

- advocating on behalf of a client.

Chapter 2

Understanding Substance Use Problems

Note: The information in this chapter is covered in Chapters 1–3 of the Client Workbook.

Introduction

This chapter provides a brief overview of substance use disorders so that the reader will be familiar with current trends in substance use, the importance of a positive attitude in developing a therapeutic alliance with clients who abuse substances, causes of substance use disorders, *Diagnostic and Statistical Manual of Mental Disorders, Fourth Edition* (*DSM–IV*; American Psychiatric Association, 1994) classification of substance-related disorders, specific *DSM–IV* symptoms of dependence and abuse, and problems associated with substance use disorders. The reader who wishes to learn more on any of these topics can consult the References and Suggested Additional Readings.

Definition of Substance Use Problems

A substance use problem exists when the client experiences any type of problem related to the ingestion of alcohol, tobacco, or other drugs including illicit street drugs and prescribed drugs such as painkillers or tranquilizers. These problems can be in any area of the client's functioning: medical or physical, psychological, family, interpersonal, social, academic, occupational, legal, financial, or spiritual.

Substance abuse and dependence are clinical diagnoses used when the problematic use of substances meets specific *DSM–IV* criteria.

Although any type of compound can be abused or cause physical or psychological addiction, the most commonly abused substances are generally alcohol, tobacco, and marijuana.

Types of Substances Used and Current Trends

The Epidemiologic Catchment Area (ECA) study, conducted in the 1980s by the National Institute of Health (Robins & Regier, 1991), found that 13.7% of adults in the United States met current or lifetime criteria for alcohol abuse or dependence, and 6.1% met criteria for drug abuse or dependence. Of all the disorders studied in adults, alcohol use disorders were the first most common substance use problem, and drug use disorders were the third most common substance use problem.

The majority of the 51 million smokers in the United States are dependent on tobacco. Unfortunately, tobacco problems are often totally ignored, despite the fact that tobacco dependence is associated with numerous medical problems and fatal diseases and has the highest mortality rate of all dependence disorders.

Although there is a trend toward reduced use of certain substances, data clearly indicate that many people have problems with alcohol, tobacco, and other drugs. Even though new trends emerge every several years (e.g., the recent increase in crack cocaine abuse), alcohol remains the number one mind-altering drug abused in the United States and continues to wreak havoc with the lives of many individuals and families.

Attitudes of Professionals and Therapeutic Alliance

Although knowledge and skill are important in clinical work with substance use disorders, the therapist's attitude plays a crucial role in treatment effectiveness. Unhelpful attitudes include cynicism and negativity, lack of hope for recovery, indifference, boredom, judgmental outlook, rigid adherence to one approach to recovery, and a great need to control the client. Helpful attitudes include hope and optimism for recovery, empathy, lack of anger or hostility, and flexibility in the approach to recovery. Although empathy for clients may be enhanced by the therapist's own experiences in personal recovery, treatment outcome research shows that there is no difference in effectiveness between therapists who are in recovery and those who are not.

Helpful attitudes contribute to a therapeutic alliance, a "connection" with the client that is experienced as genuine and helpful. A therapeutic alliance is facilitated when the client feels understood, accepted, liked, and respected by the therapist and develops trust. Treatment outcome is better when there is an alliance with the client. Therefore, the therapist's ability to establish and maintain a therapeutic alliance is a significant variable in treatment outcome.

Causes of Substance Use Problems

Substance use problems are caused by a number of different factors that vary from one person to the next. These include biological, psychological, and social or environmental factors.

Biological Factors

Problems with alcohol use in particular run in families, so it is thought that some individuals have a genetic predisposition to develop a problem with alcohol use. It is possible that differences in brain chemistry and metabolism exist that increase the likelihood of developing a substance use problem. Some people, for example, quickly develop a tolerance for alcohol or other drugs. Their bodies seem to "need" or "want" substances in a way that differs from the bodies of people who do not develop a substance use problem. There are controversies about biological causes of substance use disorders. For example, it is not clear if the craving or strong desire to use substances is a precondition or a conditioned effect of prolonged use. In addition, some people experience a positive physical effect from substances so that they are "reinforced" each time they ingest the substances.

Psychological Factors

Substances are often used to reduce anxiety or tension, to relax, to cope with other unpleasant feelings, or to escape. For some people, this eventually contributes to substance abuse or dependency as they get more accustomed to using alcohol or other drugs to feel better. Others have certain personality traits that make them more prone to using and subsequently abusing substances.

Social or Environmental Factors

The family and social environment in which people live influences behavior, including substance use behavior. A person's decision to use or not to use is affected by easy access to substances, pressure from peers to use, reinforcement from peers for using, observation of role models (e.g., parents) abusing substances, and standards or values learned from the community or broader culture.

Multiple Factors

A combination of factors can cause a person to develop a substance use problem. In cases of dependency, the factors that contributed to a person's initial use may be totally different from those that cause him or her to continue using. With some people the physical effects of substances may contribute primarily to their use, whereas with others psychological or social effects may be the primary factors.

Types of Substances Used

Any substance can be part of an abuse or dependency diagnosis or cause problems for the user, even if clinical criteria are not met. Alcohol and tobacco are the most commonly abused substances, followed by marijuana, cocaine and other stimulants, opiates, hallucinogens, and inhalants. Many people use or abuse a variety of substances. Although some people prefer a particular substance or type of substance, others are less discriminating and use many different substances.

Classification of Substance Use Disorders

DSM–IV includes several classifications of substance-related disorders:

- ■ *Intoxication* refers to the acute effects of excessive amounts of alcohol or drugs.

- ■ *Withdrawal* refers to a specific syndrome that develops following cessation or reduction of regular and heavy use of a substance (see Chapter 6 for a review of substance-specific withdrawal symptoms).

- ■ *Dependence and abuse* refer to physiological and behavioral symptoms caused by the substance use that lead to significant impairment or personal distress. Specific symptoms of dependence and abuse can be found in sections that follow.

Symptoms of Substance Dependence

DSM–IV has seven criteria for substance dependence that define a maladaptive pattern of substance use leading to significant impairment or personal distress. Three of the seven criteria must be met within a 12-month period for substance dependence to be diagnosed.

- *Criterion 1—tolerance.* This is the need for markedly increased amounts of the substance to achieve intoxication or the desired effect, or a markedly diminished effect with continued use of the same amount of a substance.

- *Criterion 2—withdrawal.* This is characterized by a specific withdrawal syndrome for a particular substance when the client stops completely or reduces the amount used, or the use of the same or a similar substance to relieve or avoid withdrawal symptoms.

- *Criterion 3—loss of control.* This involves taking the substance in larger amounts or over a longer period than was intended.

- *Criterion 4—inability to cut down or control substance use.* This involves a persistent desire or unsuccessful efforts to cut down or control substance use.

- *Criterion 5—preoccupation or compulsion.* This involves spending a great deal of time obtaining the substance, using the substance, or recovering from its effects.

- *Criterion 6—psychosocial impairment.* This involves reducing or giving up important social, occupational, or recreational activities because of substance use.

- *Criterion 7—continued use despite adverse effects.* This refers to continuation of substance use despite knowing that a persistent or recurrent physical or psychological problem is probably caused or exacerbated by the substance use.

DSM–IV criteria can be met with or without physiological dependence. If a client meets the first or second diagnostic criterion (tolerance or withdrawal), the diagnosis is specified "with physiological dependence." Other diagnostic specifications include early full remission, early partial remission, sustained full remission, sustained partial remission, on agonist therapy (e.g., methadone maintenance), and in a controlled environment (e.g., prison, therapeutic community, hospital).

Symptoms of Substance Abuse

A client with a pattern of substance use that does not meet the criteria for dependence but leads to significant impairment or distress is diagnosed with substance abuse if one or more of the following four *DSM–IV* criteria are met within a 12-month period.

- ■ *Criterion 1—failure to fulfill major role obligations.* This includes obligations at work, home, or school. Examples include repeated absences or poor performance at school or work, suspensions or expulsions from school, or neglect of children or household responsibilities.

- ■ *Criterion 2—use in situations in which it is physically hazardous.* This includes driving a vehicle or operating a machine when impaired by substance use.

- ■ *Criterion 3—legal problems.* This includes recurrent, substance-related legal problems such as arrests for disorderly conduct and driving under the influence of alcohol or drugs.

- ■ *Criterion 4—continued use despite problems.* This involves the continued use of substances despite persistent or recurrent social or interpersonal problems, such as marital conflict or physical fights, that are caused or exacerbated by the substance use.

Harmful Consequences

Substance use can contribute directly and indirectly to a multiplicity of problems in any area of functioning. Substance abuse and dependence raise the risk of medical, psychological, psychiatric, family, and economic problems. As shown in Figure 2.1, substance use problems can be classified along a continuum from mild to life-threatening. Accidents, injuries, diseases, suicides, and homicides make substance abuse or dependence fatal for many. The severity of problems varies among individuals and among the different areas of a client's functioning. Sometimes, the adverse effects of substance use can be subtle or hidden. For example, an attorney with alcohol dependence initially reported that her work was not affected by her drinking. However, upon close examination with her therapist, she discovered that her billable hours had actually decreased by about 15% as her drinking worsened.

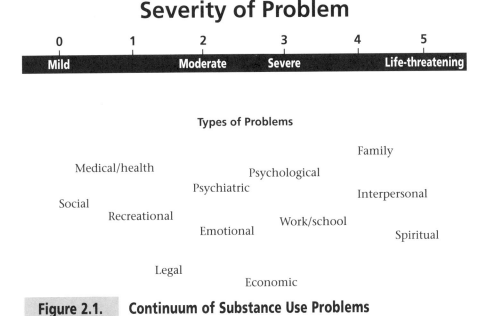

Figure 2.1. **Continuum of Substance Use Problems**

Table 2.1 summarizes some of the more common problems reported in the clinical and research literature as well as problems that clients have reported to us during assessment or treatment sessions. The number and severity of problems associated with substance use disorders will vary dramatically among clients. Also, it isn't unusual for a client, even one who is mandated to attend treatment by the court system or by an employer, to actually minimize adverse affects of substance use. Therefore, the clinician should not expect the client to be forthcoming with substance use problems in the initial sessions. Although psychological defenses may account for denial or minimization, some clients have never examined their problems closely enough to know that they were caused or worsened by substance use.

Perceived Positive Effects of Substances

Despite the problems caused by substance use, clients perceive many positive benefits. Such positive expectancies are closely linked to psychological dependence on substances. These include euphorigenic and relaxation effects, in which clients enjoy the euphoria or the "high"

Table 2.1. Problems Associated With Substance Use Disorders

Type of Problem	Example
Medical/health	accidents; injuries; poor nutrition; weight gain or loss; poor dental hygiene; increased risk of liver, heart, kidney, or lung diseases; cancers of the mouth or pharynx; gastritis; edema; high blood pressure; sexual dysfunction; complications with menstrual cycle, pregnancy, or childbirth; increased risk of AIDS; premature death
Emotional	anxiety; panic reactions; depression; mood swings; psychosis; suicidal thoughts, feelings, or behaviors; unpredictable behaviors; aggressiveness; violence; self-harm; feelings of shame and guilt; low self-esteem
Work/school	poor performance; lost jobs or dropping out of school; missing work or school; being undependable and less effective; loss of interest; ruined career; lost opportunities
Family	lost relationships due to separation, divorce, or involvement of child welfare agencies; family distress and conflict; damaged family relationships; emotional burden on the family (anger, hurt, distrust, fear, worry, depression); poor communication
Interpersonal	lost or damaged friendships; interpersonal conflicts and dissatisfaction; loss of trust or respect of significant others
Recreational	diminished interest in or loss of important hobbies, avocations, or other leisure activities
Legal	fines; legal constraints; arrests; convictions; jail or prison time; probation or parole

Table 2.1.	**Problems Associated With Substance Use Disorders** (*continued*)

Type of Problem	Example
Economic	loss of income; excessive debts; loan defaults or ignoring other financial obligations; loss of security or living arrangements; inability to take care of basic needs for food or shelter; using up all financial resources; inability to manage money

of the substance as well as the feeling of being "chilled out" or relaxed after using. Some clients also report feeling more energetic, interpersonally attractive, sexual, perceptive, or creative as a result of their substance use. Others perceive the benefits of substance use in terms of helping them blot out or escape from their problems or numb their uncomfortable feelings. Even when there are many adverse effects, clients will be able to articulate perceived positive effects of using substances, which reinforces continued use. Understanding substance use from the client's perspective helps the therapist or counselor be sensitive to the client's perceived positive benefits of using. The Decision-Making Matrix in Chapter 7 (see Figure 7.1 in Chapter 7 of this guide and Chapter 5 in the Client Workbook) provides one clinical tool for helping clients identify both positive and negative aspects of substance use.

Effects of Substance Use Problems on the Family

Alcohol and drug problems often have a negative effect on the family. Family relationships are lost due to separation, divorce, or the involvement of child welfare agencies. Families feel neglected, and in some cases their basic needs for food, shelter, and clothing are ignored. The economic burden can be tremendous as a result of large amounts of family income going for the purchase of drugs or alcohol; lost income due to impairment caused by substance use; and costs associated with legal, medical, or psychiatric problems. Family members often feel an emotional burden as well. Anger, fear, worry, distrust, and depression are common. Episodes of neglect, abuse, or violence are often associated with alcohol and other drug abuse. Substance abuse makes it difficult if not impossible to function responsibly as a parent or spouse, which leads to problems in specific family relationships. Due to the genetic predisposition associated with substance use disorders and faulty role modeling, children of parents who have alcohol or drug problems are more vulnerable than other children to developing their own substance use problems.

Case Examples

The following cases provide specific examples of alcohol abuse, tobacco and alcohol dependence, and opiate dependence with polydrug abuse. These brief cases illustrate how substance use disorders vary in terms of symptoms, severity, and adverse effects on the client and family.

Randy (Alcohol Abuse)

Randy is a 41-year-old, married father of two with a 16-year history of alcohol use. He owns a small home improvement business and employs four other men. Randy had his first drink at age 15 and first became intoxicated at age 17. He drank moderately until his early 30s, at which time he increased the frequency and amount of alcohol intake from several drinks per month to regular weekend use of six or more beers, and occasional weekday use of four or more beers, per drinking occasion. During the past year and a half, Randy has had several weekend binges leading to bad hangovers, causing him to miss work and pay less attention to his business than usual. He and his wife have begun arguing over his alcohol use and his failure to spend time with her and the children on weekends. Often on weekends, after going to potential customers' homes to give estimates, Randy stops at local bars and clubs and drinks with his friends.

Louise (Tobacco and Alcohol Dependence)

Louise is a 55-year-old, divorced mother of two adult children and grandmother of five. She had over a 30-year history of alcohol dependence. She drank on a daily basis, consuming up to a case of beer at a time during her worst period of drinking. Her tolerance was quite high for many years, although in the final years of drinking, her tolerance actually decreased. She also experienced withdrawal tremors and often drank in the morning to stop them. Her alcohol use contributed to severe family conflict, an inability to function as an effective mother when her children were young, financial problems, depression, suicidal feelings, and an inability to hold a job. Louise has been sober for over 1 year, and her life has improved modestly. She now wants to address her dependence on nicotine. Louise has been smoking two to three packs of cigarettes a day for "too many years to count." She reports that her dependence on nicotine has caused her to have problems with shortness of breath when she walks long distances or up stairs; has made her more susceptible to a variety of minor physical ailments; has been a factor in heated arguments with one of her adult sons, who refuses to bring his children to visit her "smoke-filled house"; and is using up too much of her limited income.

Steve (Opiate Dependence and Polydrug Abuse)

Steve is a 36-year-old, divorced physician who began using alcohol and marijuana during high school. His use increased during college and medical school, but he managed to make excellent grades, mainly due to his intellectual ability. During the latter part of his medical internship, Steve began snorting heroin and cocaine occasionally. This pattern continued fairly steadily when he joined a medical practice. During the past several years, Steve has prescribed himself narcotics and used these on a daily basis. He also began shooting heroin intravenously and couldn't function without opiates in his system. Steve used a variety of other drugs including marijuana, Valium™, and dalmane to treat his anxiety and insomnia and to reduce stress. Drugs eventually became the central organizing factor in his life. Prior to Steve's entering treatment involuntarily, his drug dependence cost him his marriage. To continue practicing medicine, he is required by a state regulatory agency to maintain abstinence from all illicit drugs and alcohol, participate in treatment, and submit regular urine samples to verify his abstinence.

Chapter 3

Assessment of Substance Use Problems

Areas of Assessment

The assessment of substance use problems differs from other mental health assessments in that much more detailed information is obtained on patterns of alcohol and other drug use, effects of use, potential effects of substances on other psychiatric disorders, current withdrawal potential, and attitudes and beliefs about continued use and abstinence. In addition, because intravenous drug use and other high-risk behaviors are common among clients with substance use disorders, detailed information on HIV status is sought. Emphasis is also placed on evaluating the client's social support system because of the potential detrimental effect of a negative social network (e.g., being closely connected with others who have active substance use disorders) on attempts to stop using substances or prevent a relapse. The following sections cover areas that should be assessed.

Pattern of Substance Use

The therapist should determine the client's current (past several months) and historical pattern of substance use (amount and frequency of use in each category of substances), methods of use (e.g., intravenous, intramuscular, intranasal, oral), periods of non-use or non-problematic use, and perceived reasons for using alcohol or other drugs. The therapist should also inquire about how the client acquires substances, how much money is spent on them, the interpersonal and social context of substance use, and whether the client mixes substances to "boost" the effects. If the client injects drugs, the therapist should ask if he or she shares needles, cotton, or rinsing water with other drug users, as sharing any of these items increases the chances of acquiring or transmitting the AIDS virus.

Symptoms of Substance Use Disorders

The therapist should determine how the substance use pattern presented relates to the *DSM–IV* symptoms of various disorders (abuse, dependence, withdrawal, etc.). Is there evidence of tolerance or physical withdrawal, obsessions or compulsions to use, or psychosocial impairment?

Effects of Substance Use

The therapist should ask the client about problems caused or worsened by substance use or related behaviors. These problems may be in any area of functioning: medical or physical, psychological or emotional, work or school, family, interpersonal, recreational, legal, spiritual, or economic. In the initial assessment period, the client is often not aware of or minimizes the adverse effects of substance use on self and others. The therapist may identify more specific effects in subsequent assessment and treatment sessions by having the client complete the Harmful Effects Worksheet (see Figure 3.1 in this guide and Chapter 3 in the Client Workbook), which asks the client to list problems caused by substance use as they relate to every major domain of functioning.

Psychological or Psychiatric Problems

The therapist should find out if the client is currently experiencing serious psychiatric or psychological problems such as depression; mania; anxiety; phobias; obsessions or compulsions; psychosis; suicidal thoughts; homicidal thoughts; self-destructive behaviors (e.g., cutting or burning self); violent aggressive behaviors; problems with compulsive eating, gambling, or sex; or problems with bingeing and purging. The therapist should also find out if the client is experiencing any upsetting feelings resulting from prior traumatic experiences, such as being a victim of incest, sexual abuse, or violence or witnessing unusual events such as combat or horrible disasters. If symptoms or problems are currently endorsed, the therapist should ask how long they have been present and how much they bother the client in order to determine subjective distress. The therapist should ask the client how his or her substance use affects the symptoms and how he or she thinks the symptoms affect substance use. Is there any family history of psychiatric illness or any prior treatment received by the client for a non-substance use problem (e.g., inpatient psychiatric hospital, partial hospital program, community residential program, outpatient therapy, pharmacotherapy)? What did the client find helpful or unhelpful about prior treatment experiences?

Problems Caused by or Worsened by Your Substance Use

Instructions: In the sections below, list any problems that you think were caused by or worsened by your alcohol, tobacco, or drug problem in the past year. Then, rank each of the eight categories from the most severe to the least severe, using "1" for the most severe category of problems.

Medical/physical/dental	*Lost weight*
5	*Poor dental hygiene*
	Hurt in auto accident and a fall

| **Psychological or emotional** | *Felt like a nobody* |
| 1 | *Depressed* |

Work/school	*Work at 80% capacity*
4	*Used all my sick days up*
	Quit night school, didn't get my degree

| **Family** | *Wife and kids are upset and disappointed in me* |
| 2 | *Parents are heartbroken* |

| **Interpersonal relationships** | *Friend, John, upset with me* |
| 7 | |

| **Recreational** | *Bored with events where I couldn't drink* |
| 8 | *Gave up playing sports* |

| **Legal** | *Charged with driving under the influence of alcohol* |
| 3 | |

Economic	*Spent too much money to count on booze*
6	*Created financial problems for family*
	Never saved for the future

Figure 3.1.   Example of Completed Harmful Effects Worksheet

Medical and Sexual History

The therapist should ask about current or past medical or dental problems, medications currently used, allergies, or adverse reactions to any medications. Is there any significant family medical history? What is the client's sexual preference? Is there any history of sexual problems or high-risk behaviors, such as intravenous drug use, that increase the client's chances of being HIV-positive?

Psychosocial History

The therapist should inquire about the client's relationships with family (parents and siblings, spouse, children) and friends. The therapist should also ask about the client's academic, work, financial, and legal histories; hobbies and avocations; and religious preferences.

Motivation to Change

The therapist should inquire why the client is seeking help and what the client wants to change about his or her substance use. Motivation may be external (e.g., legal system, employer, family, significant other), internal, or a combination of both. Clients often initially seek help as a result of some external pressure. As part of the initial assessment, the client should complete the Self-Rating Scale (see Figure 3.2 in this guide and Chapter 2 in the Client Workbook). On the Self-Rating Scale, the client rates the severity of the substance use problem and the level of his or her motivation to quit substance use. The therapist should determine which stage of change the client is in (precontemplation, contemplation, preparation, action, maintenance, or termination; see Chapter 7 for information on these stages).

Past History of Treatment and Use of Self-Help Programs

The therapist should gather information about the client's prior involvement in any type of substance abuse treatment (e.g., detoxification; inpatient or outpatient rehabilitation program; partial hospital or intensive outpatient program; therapeutic community; halfway house; outpatient or aftercare counseling; self-help groups such as Alcoholics Anonymous, Narcotics Anonymous, Cocaine Anonymous, Rational Recovery, Self-Management and Recovery Training, Women for Sobriety, Moderation Management, or any other self-help program). What is the client's perception of the effectiveness of prior treatments, and what did the client find helpful or unhelpful? The therapist should

Instructions: After reviewing your pattern of substance use and the consequences, rate the current severity of your problem. Then rate your current level of motivation to quit using substances.

Severity Level of My Problem

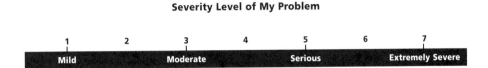

My Motivation Level to Quit Using Substances

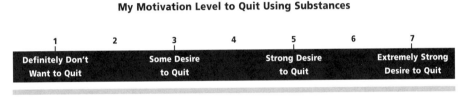

| Figure 3.2. | Self-Rating Scale |

also inquire about the client's past use of pharmacotherapeutic agents for detoxification or ongoing treatment (e.g., methadone, naltrexone, bromocriptine, amantadine, disulfiram).

History of Attempts to Quit Without Help

The therapist should ask the client about past attempts at quitting substance use without help. Many clients have quit cigarette, alcohol, or drug use on their own without the help of professionals, medications, or self-help groups. If the client did quit without help, what cognitive, behavioral, or other strategies did he or she use?

Coping Skills

The therapist should assess the client's style of coping with problems, stress, and upsetting feelings. Does the client blame others for his or her difficulties or accept responsibility? Does the client cope with distress by using alcohol or other drugs? What kinds of cognitive strategies does the client typically use (e.g., self-reflection, challenging and changing beliefs or thinking, positive self-talk)? What behavioral strategies does the client usually use (e.g., avoidance, testing out new behaviors, monitoring specific behaviors or actions)? What interpersonal tactics does the client use (e.g., reaching out for social support, sharing problems and feelings with a confidant, talking through problems at self-help meetings)? What spiritual strategies does the client use (e.g., prayer, meditation, participation in formal religious activities)?

Social Support System

The therapist should assess whether the client has supportive family or friends. Does he or she have one or more confidants? Are current relationships satisfying? Is the client able to give and receive support from significant others and manage interpersonal conflict? Is the client involved with a partner or friends who actively abuse alcohol or other drugs? Does the client have significant others who are not likely to exert pressure to use alcohol or drugs?

Methods of Assessment

To complete the assessment, therapists can use clinical or collateral interviews, pen-and-paper tests, urinalysis or breathalyzer screenings, laboratory tests, or prior treatment records. Specific methods used depend on the therapist's preferences, the reason the client is seeking help, and the system in which the therapist works. Supplemental sources of information such as laboratory tests and collateral interviews are especially helpful when the client is perceived not to be providing accurate information.

Clinical Interviews

Clinical interviews can be conducted with structured instruments such as the Addiction Severity Index (ASI; McLellan et al., 1986). In addition to a baseline ASI, there are 7-day and 30-day versions that can be used to assess the client at various points in the treatment process. Clinical interviews can also be semi-structured, covering a broad range of areas such as those discussed in the previous section.

Collateral Interviews

It is sometimes helpful and necessary to gather additional information from people who are familiar with the client and his or her problems. Family members, significant others, or professionals (e.g., probation officer, family physician) may provide important information about

the client. Collateral interviews are often helpful when the client
is seeking help for an external reason. Due to stringent federal and state
confidentiality guidelines related to releasing information on clients with
alcohol or other drug problems, the therapist must first get the client's
written permission to obtain information from or share information with
family, significant others, prior counselors or therapists, or others
involved with the client (e.g., criminal justice, social service, or health
care professionals).

Pen-and-Paper Tests

Brief questionnaires such as the *Michigan Alcoholism Screening Test* (MAST;
Selzer, 1971) or *Drug Abuse Screening Test* (DAST; Skinner, 1982) can
be used to supplement data gained from clinical interviews. More
comprehensive questionnaires, such as the *Drug Use Screening
Inventory* (DUSI; Tarter, 1990; Tarter & Hegedus, 1991; Tarter, Ott,
& Mezzich, 1991) can be used to gather more detailed information
to use in prioritizing problems and determining treatment needs
of a client. There are also questionnaires that help measure treatment
readiness, risk for AIDS, cravings for substances, and involvement
in self-help programs. Although these and other questionnaires
are often used in treatment-research clinical trials, they can be helpful
to the therapist as well. It is most appropriate to administer these
questionnaires during the assessment process, as they can be used
by the treating therapist to provide feedback to the client. Questionnaires
such as the MAST, DAST, DUSI, or "Risk for AIDS" (Lis & Mercer, 1994)
can be used with all clients who are entering treatment for substance
use problems for the first time. Questionnaires that focus on specific
recovery issues such as cravings or use of self-help programs can
be administered at various points during treatment (e.g., every 30
or 60 days and at the end of treatment).

Urinalysis and Breathalyzer Screenings

Urinalysis and breathalyzer screenings can be used during the initial
assessment, regularly, or as needed throughout the course of treatment,
or randomly. This type of screening helps determine recent use
of substances, helps monitor the client's progress in treatment or difficulty
staying sober, and provides an external control for abstinence that many
clients find helpful. Regular urinalysis and breathalyzer screenings can
be especially helpful in eliminating controversy over whether a specific
client who was mandated for treatment has used substances. For example,
health care professionals, athletes, attorneys, bus drivers, court-mandated
clients, and others who are mandated for treatment are frequently

required to submit regular urine samples as a way of monitoring sobriety. These screenings can actually protect such individuals in the event they are falsely accused of using substances. There are various types of tests available, including thin-layer chromatography (TLC), enzyme immunoassay (EIA), enzyme multiplied immunoassay test (EMIT), radioimmunoassay (RIA), fluorescent polarization immunoassay (FPIA), and gas-liquid chromatography (GLC).

Laboratory Tests

Laboratory tests can be used to help screen for alcohol problems because serum assays can be elevated by excessive drinking. However, problem drinkers can have normal scores, so a normal score cannot be interpreted as an absence of physical damage from drinking. Tests such as plasma y-glutamyl transferase (GGT) and mean corpuscular volume (MSV) measure injury to the liver and the cells that manufacture red blood cells. Other tests such as the plasma carbohydrate-deficient transferrin (CDT) measure nonspecific alcohol-related changes rather than organ damage. An HIV test, a hepatitis antigen and antibody test, or other tests (e.g., pregnancy test, tuberculin skin test, chest X-ray) may be used based on the circumstances of the client.

Prior Treatment Records

Records of previous treatment experiences or records from other significant sources (e.g., probation officer, EAP evaluator) can provide additional information about the client.

Client's Choice of Treatment Goals

Note: Treatment goals are covered in Chapters 4 and 7 of the Client Workbook.

Treatment goals need to be negotiated with each client. They are based on current problems, motivation to change, and perceived needs for treatment. In many instances the assessment will provide sufficient information to document a severe substance dependence or abuse problem. In these cases abstinence should be encouraged by the clinician even if the client does not agree with this goal. In such cases, the clinician can provide specific feedback as to why abstinence is recommended. However, there will be instances in which a client doesn't meet the criteria for substance abuse or dependency yet is having some problems with substance use. Although many clients will identify abstinence from substances as their desired goal, others may prefer only to reduce their harmful use of substances. Some clients will successfully learn to moderate their use, but others will learn that they cannot do this for an extended period of time.

Case Examples

The following cases provide examples of three different individuals who sought treatment for problems with alcohol or other drugs. These cases clearly illustrate that the actual effects of substance use problems may vary significantly among individuals.

Tracy (Mild Effects)

Tracy is a 28-year-old, married, employed mother of two children who has a 6-year history of alcohol and marijuana abuse. Tracy is in good physical health and has had no major problems from her substance use. However, she reports that her occasional bouts of intoxication lead to arguments with her husband and that she feels guilty for embarrassing herself and her family. Tracy also was involved in a minor car accident while under the influence of marijuana.

Don (Moderate Effects)

Don is a 49-year-old college professor and married father of two adult children. He has had an alcohol problem for the past 10 years and has twice successfully completed rehabilitation programs leading to periods of abstinence for several years or longer. His most recent relapse came after 30 months of continuous sobriety. Although he is tenured at the college where he teaches, he feels pressure to maintain his sobriety because his last binge affected his ability to teach, and the dean of his department pressured him to seek professional help again. Don reports that his wife is worried about and upset with him and his adult children are disappointed that he relapsed. He feels guilty and ashamed that he had to return to treatment after doing so well for several years. Don's latest relapse was also a factor in an episode of depression.

George (Severe Effects)

George is a 41-year-old, unemployed, divorced father of three children who has a 23-year history of alcoholism, heroin dependence, tobacco dependence, and crack cocaine abuse. George's wife left him over 15 years ago after he was arrested and spent time in jail for burglary. He became involved in crime at that time to support an expensive daily heroin addiction. Although George has not used any opiate drugs in the past 11 years, his drinking has increased considerably. More recently, he also started using crack cocaine. George states that his addiction has led to many serious problems in his life. These include losing several relationships with women; being a victim of robbery and violent beatings on at least three occasions; getting kicked out of apartments many times, leading to periods of homelessness; poor nutrition, leading to loss of weight, dental problems, and poor physical health; gastritis caused by excessive drinking; gout; chronic obstructive pulmonary disease caused by excessive smoking; losing many jobs and being unable to work; and numerous arrests for public intoxication and two arrests for selling drugs. George has been in jail several times, hospitalized for complications of his alcoholism four times, hospitalized in a psychiatric facility twice following suicidal feelings after going on crack cocaine runs, detoxified in hospitals and Salvation Army social detoxification centers more than 20 times, and treated in addiction rehabilitation programs and halfway house programs at least five times. Whereas once he maintained continuous sobriety for over 2 years, the longest he has been able to stay sober in the past 5 years has been 3 months.

Part 2

Treatment Settings and Approaches

Chapter 4

Treatment Settings for Substance Use Problems

Note: The information in this chapter is covered in Chapter 4 of the Client Workbook.

Introduction

Effective work with clients who have substance use problems requires the therapist to be aware of and able to use a broad range of treatment resources. In this chapter, a range of treatment settings is briefly discussed.

In general, the least restrictive level of treatment should be used unless the severity of the substance use disorder and related medical, psychiatric, and social problems are such that structured or medically monitored treatment is needed. Therapists are encouraged to become conversant with the American Society on Addiction Medicine (ASAM) criteria (Hoffman, Halikas, Mee-Lee, & Weedman, 1991) so they can make appropriate decisions on what level of care to seek for a given client. ASAM delineates four levels of care:

- Level 1—outpatient treatment

- Level 2—intensive outpatient treatment

- Level 3—medically monitored intensive inpatient treatment

- Level 4—medically managed intensive inpatient treatment

ASAM uses specific criteria along six different dimensions to determine the most appropriate level of care. These dimensions are acute intoxication and/or withdrawal potential, biomedical conditions and complications, emotional or behavioral conditions and complications, treatment acceptance or resistance, relapse potential, and recovery environment.

Outpatient and Aftercare Programs (Level 1)

These programs vary in length of treatment from several weeks to months or longer. They may precede or follow rehabilitation treatment programs or be used as the sole treatment. Their purpose is to help the client achieve and maintain abstinence or reduce harmful substance use, as well as make personal changes to facilitate ongoing recovery and minimize relapse risk. Individual, group, and family therapy; pharmacotherapy; and other ancillary services may be offered, depending on the specific outpatient or aftercare setting. Outpatient treatment is most suitable for clients who are not at risk for withdrawal complications, have a stable medical condition, show a willingness to cooperate with treatment, are able to maintain abstinence with minimal support, and have a supportive recovery environment.

Nonresidential Addiction Rehabilitation Programs (Level 2)

These short-term (2–6 week) programs include intensive outpatient and partial hospital programs. These programs provide addiction and recovery education and treatment to clients who do not need the supervision and structure of a residential program. These are sometimes used as "step-down" programs for clients who have received treatment in residential addiction programs or as "step-up" programs for clients who started treatment in a more traditional outpatient program but were unable to make sufficient progress. These programs are appropriate for clients who have minimal withdrawal risk, have no serious medical conditions, have enough resistance to recovery to require a structured treatment program, are likely to relapse without close monitoring and support, and have an unsupportive environment.

Inpatient Hospital and Residential Rehabilitation Programs (Levels 3 and 4)

Although managed care has led to a significant decrease in the availability of inpatient and residential programs for substance use disorders, a wide range of options is still available. Options include both hospital based and non-hospital based residential programs. Some are "generic" in the sense that as long as a client meets the program's criteria, he or she can be admitted to the program. Others are highly specialized and serve specific populations based on type and severity of addiction, gender, family status, or ethnicity. Following is a brief description of inpatient programs.

Short-Term Addiction Rehabilitation Programs

The prototypical 28-day rehabilitation program has changed drastically. Most programs now offer a variable length of stay, with many clients staying only 7 to 14 days. Unless there are serious, substance-related medical or psychiatric problems, non-hospital based rehabilitation programs are the first choice. Addiction rehabilitation programs are usually recommended if clients have been unable to initiate and sustain recovery through less intensive treatment settings such as outpatient, intensive outpatient, or partial hospital programs. They may also be used if the addiction is of such severity that a period of time in a structured, residential setting is needed to break the cycle of addiction and help motivate the client to establish a foundation for recovery. Short-term rehabilitation programs are also appropriate for clients who have high relapse potential, who are in environments considered dangerous for recovery, or who do not have access to outpatient rehabilitation.

Long-Term Addiction Rehabilitation Programs

Some clients with severe patterns of addiction and serious psychosocial impairment (e.g., no social support, lack of vocational skills, history of multiple relapses, serious problems with the legal system) need long-term programs (several months to a year or longer) to maintain sobriety and address important lifestyle and personality issues. Long-term rehabilitation programs include therapeutic communities; halfway houses; and specialized programs for designated populations such as men, women, women with children, specific ethnic groups, and clients involved with the criminal justice system as a result of their substance use. The trend is toward shorter programs. For example, therapeutic community programs that were once up to 2 years in length are now several months to less than a year in duration.

Detoxification (Levels 3 and 4)

Detoxification refers to the process of tapering the client off of alcohol or other drugs. Medical detoxification may be provided in an addiction rehabilitation facility, psychiatric hospital, or medical hospital. Medical detoxification is indicated if there is a documented history or current evidence of withdrawal complications such as seizures, delirium tremens (DTs), or serious suicidal feelings. In contemporary practice, medical detoxification normally takes up to several days. Detoxification from severe dependence on opiates or benzodiazepines may be initiated in a detoxification program, continued in outpatient or partial hospital treatment, and last several weeks or longer.

Some clients benefit from "social detoxification" programs in which supportive care, rest, and nutrition are offered. Referrals are made to medical facilities in cases of complicated withdrawal. Social detoxification programs are usually provided for chronic substance users from lower socioeconomic groups.

Recently, emphasis has been placed on outpatient detoxification. This is appropriate for clients with less severe forms of substance use disorders who do not show any evidence of serious substance-related medical or psychiatric problems and who have support from family or other significant people.

In general, detoxification involves providing medications to attenuate withdrawal symptoms. Detoxification is of limited value if not followed by other forms of treatment such as rehabilitation or outpatient care. Although there is not a standard approach to detoxification, specific protocols do exist that outline when to use, increase, or decrease medication. Chapter 6 provides information on medications used in detoxification from different substances.

Special Programs

Other specialized treatment programs include those designed specifically for smoking cessation, those designed as part of a treatment-research protocol to study a specific type of outpatient psychosocial treatment (e.g., coping skills training, relapse prevention) or pharmacotherapy, or those designed for clients with dual disorders (e.g., substance use and psychiatric disorders).

Methadone Maintenance

Methadone maintenance (MM) is used to help opiate addicts who have been unsuccessful in their attempts to quit. Provided in conjunction with education and counseling services, MM is designed to help wean the client from opiates. However, many clients actually remain on MM for many months, even years. MM helps reduce use of illicit opiates and related criminal behavior, and helps opiate addicts function at work and in the community. Despite criticisms, MM is a helpful treatment for addicts who are unable to sustain abstinence from heroin or other opiate drugs.

Chapter 5

Psychosocial Therapies for Substance Use Disorders

Introduction

There are a variety of psychosocial therapies and counseling approaches for alcohol, tobacco, and other drug problems. Although some specific treatments have been shown in clinical trials to be more effective than others, to date there is no single, superior treatment approach appropriate for all clients. For example, in a large-scale, multi-site study of clients with alcohol problems who were randomly assigned to one of three treatment approaches (cognitive-behavioral coping skills training, motivational enhancement therapy, and 12-step facilitation counseling), it was found that all treatments worked similarly (Project MATCH Research Group, 1997). Although clients benefited from all three of these psychosocial treatments, none was significantly superior to the others. All three treatments were provided by trained counselors using a manual-based treatment approach.

Different types of individuals respond to different treatment approaches. Although brief treatments have been successful with less severe types of alcohol problems, longer-term treatments are often needed for drug problems. For many clients, substance use is a chronic disorder requiring long-term involvement in professional treatment, self-help programs, or both.

In recent years, a number of specific individual and group treatment approaches have been described in treatment manuals. Most of these manuals were initially developed for use in clinical trials and describe the theoretical orientation of the treatment approach, clinical techniques, and recovery issues to address in individual or group sessions.

The following list of psychosocial treatments shows that there
are many different approaches currently used to treat substance
use problems. Although a discussion of these various treatment
approaches is beyond the scope of this guide, the interested reader
is encouraged to consult one of the major reviews of treatments
for substance use disorders such as the *Practice Guidelines for the Treatment
of Patients with Substance Use Disorders: Alcohol, Cocaine, Opioids* (American
Psychiatric Association, 1995), recently published as a supplement
to *The American Journal of Psychiatry*. Other resources are listed
in the Suggested Additional Readings.

Psychosocial therapies and approaches

Cognitive and behavioral therapies

Coping and social skills training

Dual disorder (substance use and psychiatric
disorders) therapies

Dynamic and interpersonal therapies

Family and marital therapies

Harm reduction

Cue exposure and extinction

Group therapies

Motivational enhancement therapy

Neurobehavioral model of recovery

Relapse prevention

Social network therapy

12-step facilitation therapy

Treatment Principles and Guidelines

Following is a brief summary of important treatment principles and guidelines that can serve as a general framework for dealing with substance use disorders. These are based on a review of the literature and the authors' combined experience providing direct clinical care.

1. *Assessment.* A thorough assessment is needed to determine specific problems and treatment goals. A variety of assessment strategies can be used to complete a detailed evaluation of each client who is seeking treatment (see Chapter 3).

2. *Treatment settings.* There are a variety of treatment settings available for substance use problems. Whereas some clients participate in a single type of treatment setting, others move among many settings. In general, the least restrictive level of care should be used when feasible. Inpatient programs, for example, should not be routinely used before other levels of treatment have been tried unless the severity of the substance use disorder and concomitant medical or psychiatric problems warrant inpatient care (see Chapter 4).

3. *Therapeutic alliance.* Establishing and maintaining a therapeutic alliance is essential in helping the client adhere to the treatment plan. The clinician must be aware of both helpful and unhelpful attitudes and behaviors that affect the therapeutic alliance with substance users.

4. *Client motivation.* Because clients are often reluctant to enter treatment, the clinician needs to have strategies to motivate them to enter and remain in treatment. Many clients enter treatment as a result of external motivation or pressure. Outreach efforts are often needed to reengage those who terminate treatment prematurely.

5. *Flexibility.* A flexible approach to treatment is needed. If one type of program or intervention is minimally effective or ineffective, other approaches should be considered. Psychosocial, pharmacologic, and self-help programs all are valuable treatments for substance use problems. Changes should be made to a particular treatment based on the client's progress or lack of progress.

6. *Treatment modalities.* A single type of treatment is seldom effective. Often, clients need a combination of treatments such as therapy and self-help meetings or therapy, medications, and self-help meetings.

7. *Treatment phases.* There are different phases or stages of recovery from a substance use disorder. Recovery is not a linear process, so clients do not go smoothly from one phase to the next. Additionally, because many clients lapse or relapse, they move back and forth between the phases. The stages of change paradigm is a broad framework that considers time in treatment and specific recovery issues. The goals of treatment will change depending on which stage a client is in and the specific problems and challenges he or she is facing (see Chapter 7).

8. *Treatment issues.* Recovery is a process that involves change in substance use and in other areas of functioning. The specific changes that each client attempts to make may occur in any major domain of functioning: physical, emotional, family, social or interpersonal, spiritual, and lifestyle (see Chapter 8).

9. *Coping skills.* Learning coping skills to deal with problems resulting from or contributing to substance use disorders is critical for a client's long-term success. Clients often need help in developing cognitive, behavioral, and interpersonal skills to deal with a range of recovery challenges such as cravings, upsetting feelings, interpersonal conflict, pressures to use, and early warning signs of relapse (see Chapters 9–18). Developing coping skills involves education, awareness, a lot of practice, and the ability to change ineffective coping responses. Coping is central to most cognitive-behavioral strategies, including relapse prevention responses.

10. *Holistic approach.* Treatment should reflect a consideration of the client's current and past patterns of substance use, medical and psychiatric condition, age, gender, family situation, ethnicity, and social environment. Clients with special needs (e.g., housing, vocational training, comorbid psychiatric illness) will need help addressing them, particularly when they interfere with the recovery process.

11. *Family issues.* Because substance use disorders adversely affect the family, this issue should be discussed with the client. Involving the family is often helpful to both the client and the family (see Chapter 13).

12. *Social network.* A supportive social network facilitates recovery. Helping clients evaluate and develop social supports and participate in self-help programs plays a critical role in their long-term success (see Chapters 14 and 15).

13. *Lapse and relapse.* Because lapses and relapses are common, these issues need to be addressed in order to better prepare the client to cope with high-risk situations and to minimize the adverse effects of returning to substance use (see Chapters 16 and 17).

14. *Measuring progress.* There are a variety of ways to measure progress, including cessation or reduction of substance use, reduction of biopsychosocial problems caused or worsened by substance use, and improvement in any domain of functioning. Progress is not an "all or none" phenomenon and should be measured relative to a specific client's problems and treatment goals (see Chapter 19). Treatment outcome is influenced by client variables (e.g., severity of substance use, motivation, personal resources), treatment (e.g., appropriateness, type and length of treatment), and environmental variables (e.g., family and social supports).

Chapter 6

Medications for Substance Use Problems

Note: The information in this chapter is covered in Chapter 15 of the Client Workbook.

Withdrawing From Addictive Drugs

If the client has a physical addiction to alcohol or other drugs and has been unable to quit on his or her own, or if the client has a history of complications related to withdrawal such as seizures, delirium tremens (DTs), severe depression, or suicidal feelings, detoxification in a supervised environment is needed to reduce, stop, or prevent withdrawal symptoms. Less severe forms of dependency can be managed on an outpatient basis. The following sections describe withdrawal symptoms for various substances, and medications used to help clients withdraw from the substances.

Alcohol Withdrawal

Withdrawal symptoms usually start on the first day and peak on the second or third day after completely stopping or significantly cutting down alcohol use after drinking heavily for several days or longer. Symptoms include tremors of hands, tongue, and eyelids; nausea and vomiting; weakness; sweating; elevated blood pressure or tachycardia; anxiety; depression or irritability; and orthostatic hypotension. More severe cases of withdrawal may include delusions (false beliefs), hallucinations, seizures, or agitated behavior. Alcohol withdrawal usually takes several days and may involve taking depressant medications such as Valium™, Librium™, or Serax.

Depressant Withdrawal

Heavy or prolonged use of other depressant drugs such as sedatives and tranquilizers can cause withdrawal symptoms similar to alcohol withdrawal symptoms. Withdrawal from depressant drugs is done by gradually tapering the client off the drug he or she is addicted to, or by substituting a drug that has similar actions on the central nervous system. Withdrawal from some of the longer acting tranquilizers takes more than a few days. The process may start in an inpatient setting, then continue in an outpatient setting.

Opiate or Narcotic Withdrawal

Withdrawal from opiates or narcotics after a period of heavy, prolonged use may cause symptoms such as runny nose, tearing eyes, dilated pupils, gooseflesh, sweating, diarrhea, yawning, mild hypertension, tachycardia, fever, and insomnia. Symptoms start 6 to 12 hours after the last drug dose, peak on the second or third day, and usually end in 7 to 14 days, depending on the specific opiate or narcotic used and the length of addiction. Withdrawal from heroin or other opiate or narcotic drugs involves taking methadone or clonidine.

Cocaine and Stimulant Withdrawal

Depressed mood, fatigue, disturbed sleep, and increased dreaming are symptoms associated with withdrawal from stimulant drugs after prolonged, heavy use. Although there is not a severe physical withdrawal syndrome associated with addiction to cocaine or other stimulant drugs, antidepressants and dopamine agonists are sometimes used to help the withdrawal process.

Nicotine Withdrawal

Nicotine withdrawal symptoms usually begin within hours of stopping or significantly reducing tobacco use following regular and heavy use. These symptoms include tobacco cravings, irritability, anxiety, problems concentrating, restlessness, headaches, drowsiness, and gastrointestinal disturbances. Nicotine gum or patches are used to help the client gradually withdraw from tobacco products such as cigarettes. Nicotine gum helps to minimize nicotine withdrawal symptoms and to decrease the smoker's risk of relapse in the early weeks and months of being tobacco-free. However, it can be addictive and should not be used if the client has certain medical conditions such as a recent myocardial infarction, vasospastic disease, cardiac arrythmia, esophagitis, peptic ulcers, or inflammation of the mouth or throat. Some people complain

of side effects such as hiccups, nausea, jaw irritation, and bad taste.
A nicotine patch can help stop withdrawal symptoms and decrease
tension, anxiety, irritability, restlessness, and nicotine cravings.
The patch gradually releases nicotine into the system, usually over
a period of 24 hours. It can be used up to several weeks or longer.

Nicotine nasal sprays and nicotine inhalers are two other approaches
used to help people stop smoking by decreasing the urge to smoke.
Nicotine replacement allows the client to deal with the psychological,
social, and behavioral aspects of the nicotine habit without having
to simultaneously deal with the physical addiction. This strategy is most
effective when used in conjunction with a behavior change program.

Case Example: Lorraine (Nicotine Patch)

Lorraine is a 58-year-old teacher with a 35-year history of dependence
on cigarettes. She quit smoking on her own many times, but always
relapsed within several weeks. Lorraine was smoking nearly three packs
a day when she decided to try a nicotine patch rather than quit "cold
turkey." Over the course of a month, Lorraine was able to stop cigarettes
completely. She has been smoke-free for 9 months. She reports occasional
cravings but feels she's able to talk herself out of wanting to smoke.
Lorraine also exercises regularly and has learned some ways to reduce
stress in her life so she is not as likely to smoke to cope with stress.

Maintaining Abstinence From Addictive Drugs

Abstinence From Alcohol

Disulfiram, known by the trade name Antabuse, is a drug used by some
clients to help "buy time" when they want to drink. Antabuse stays
in the system for a week or longer, so if the client decides to drink,
he or she has to wait for the Antabuse to clear the system to avoid getting
sick. If the client ingests any alcohol while Antabuse is in his or her
system, the client will get sick because Antabuse interrupts the body's
normal process of metabolizing alcohol. The idea behind this drug
is simple: it will hopefully deter the client from using any alcohol, but
if the client does drink and get sick, the punishment will deter him or her
from drinking in the future. Antabuse usually is recommended only
for the short term, (6 months or less), due to its effects on the liver.
Also, a fatal reaction can occur if someone drinks while on Antabuse,
so it is not recommended for the impulsive client.

Naltrexone was initially developed for use with people addicted to heroin or other opiate drugs, to block the euphoric effects of these drugs. More recently, this medication has been used with alcoholics. Known by the trade name ReVia, naltrexone appears to block the effects of the body's own opioids, which reduces the reinforcing properties of alcohol and thus the desire to drink. ReVia cannot be used if the client is currently using any narcotic drugs or if he or she has hepatitis or liver disease.

Case Example: Christina (Naltrexone)

Christina is a 38-year-old attorney with a very long history of alcohol dependence. Although she had been in numerous treatment programs in the past and had participated in AA meetings, the longest she had ever been sober was 5 weeks. Christina returned to outpatient treatment as a result of a DWI charge. Given her strong cravings for alcohol and inability to stay sober with other treatments, Christina agreed to use naltrexone and attend therapy sessions twice per week. She has now been sober for over 7 months and strongly believes that ReVia (naltrexone) has helped her recovery. Christina has also been able to decrease the frequency of her therapy sessions.

Abstinence From Opiates

Drugs such as Trexan or LAAM are opiate antagonists that block the euphoric effects of heroin or other opiate drugs. This type of drug reduces the client's desire to continue using opiates.

Some clients who are dependent on heroin or other opiate drugs have an extremely difficult time staying drug-free, even after participating in rehabilitation or other treatment programs. Methadone maintenance (MM) is a treatment in which use of heroin or other opiate drugs is stopped and methadone, a longer-acting opiate, is substituted. Regular doses of methadone help the addicted person avoid using heroin or other opiates. Very importantly, MM enables the addicted person to resume normal life activities, such as work. Although intended as an interim treatment of a few months to a year or two, some clients will continue to use MM for many years. Methadone can be given only at specially licensed clinics. Both public and private MM clinics are available.

Case Example: Patrick (Methadone Maintenance)

Patrick is a 34-year-old nurse whose addiction to heroin has caused him to lose a marriage; get fired from one job; and experience numerous other legal, emotional, and financial problems. Although he had been through detoxification and had participated in several rehabilitation programs, outpatient therapy, and NA, he was unable to stay drug-free for longer than a few months until he got into an MM program. Patrick has not used heroin or any other drugs or alcohol in almost 2 years. He has been able to return to gainful employment and feels his life is much improved. Talking about daily hassles and stresses with his MM counselor helps Patrick keep from using alcohol or other drugs.

Abstinence From Cocaine

Drugs such as bromocriptine or amantadine are sometimes used to reduce a client's craving for cocaine. The results of research on their effectiveness are mixed, and they are not used in many treatment programs.

Medications for Coexisting Psychiatric Disorder

If the client suffers from a psychiatric disorder in addition to the substance use disorder, he or she may benefit from the use of medications. Psychiatric medications such as antidepressants sometimes have the added benefit of reducing the client's desire to use substances such as alcohol. However, some psychiatric medications, such as tranquilizers or sedatives, can be addictive and contribute to relapse.

Case Example: BJ (Mood Stabilizer)

BJ is a 46-year-old laborer with a long history of abuse and dependence on alcohol, marijuana, and crack cocaine. His addiction has led to many problems and played a major role in a long string of fights with other men. However, even in the absence of substance use, BJ is a violent man. After being sober for almost 2 months, he continued to experience severe mood swings with intense anger and irritability. These mood swings had always led him back to alcohol or drug use in the past. BJ was diagnosed with a mood disorder and reluctantly agreed to take Depakote, a mood stabilizer. To his surprise, he felt much better and did not impulsively return to drug use as he had in the past. For the first time in his life, BJ has been sober from both alcohol and drugs for over a year. He also reports that he hasn't been in any fights since starting the medications and feels his irritability and bad temper are now under control.

Medications as Adjunctive Versus Primary Treatments

For ongoing recovery from alcohol or other drug problems, medications should be used in conjunction with therapy or counseling, participation in self-help programs, or both. Medication has limited value if not used as an adjunctive treatment. The amount of time medications should be taken depends on the particular client's history of substance use, problems caused by it, and response to prior treatment.

How to Know if the Client Needs Medication

Medications can help when the client in recovery

- has been unable to stay off of alcohol, tobacco, or other drugs for longer than a few months at a time;
- has tried other forms of treatment and still gone back to using alcohol, tobacco, or other drugs;
- feels it is very difficult to not drink, use tobacco, or other drugs despite knowing he or she should quit and wanting to quit;
- often feels overwhelmed by cravings and strong desires to use alcohol, tobacco, or other drugs;
- has a lot to lose if he or she relapses, such as an important relationship, job, or professional status or license;
- has his or her physical health or mental stability increasingly affected by the substance use the longer use continues;
- believes his or her life would be better if he or she stayed sober from alcohol, tobacco, or other drugs; or
- believes medications will help him or her benefit more from other forms of treatment such as professional therapy or self-help groups.

Sometimes questions are raised about risks and side effects of medications. A cost-benefit analysis can help the client see the risks and benefits. Usually, the risks and costs of taking medications are small in comparison with the risks of continued abuse of or dependency on alcohol, tobacco, or other drugs.

Part 3

Change Issues and Strategies

Chapter 7

Session Topic: Stages of Change and Using Therapy or Counseling

Note: This session covers Chapters 5 and 6 in the Client Workbook.

Introduction

Clients go through different stages when they stop using substances and make personal and lifestyle changes. Whereas some clients struggle with their recovery and never progress much beyond the first stage or two, others move more easily into more advanced stages and are able to explore intrapersonal and interpersonal issues that go beyond simply staying substance-free. There are several different conceptualizations of stages of change; the interested reader is encouraged to explore these by consulting the list of Suggested Additional Readings. The authors find it helpful to use the paradigm of Prochaska, Norcross, and DiClemente (1994), which presents six stages of change: precontemplation, contemplation, preparation, action, maintenance, and termination.

1. The first stage, called *precontemplation,* is one in which the client isn't aware of a problem and is resistant to change. The client may be in denial and not see the alcohol or drug problem even if other people can.

2. The second stage is called *contemplation.* During this stage the client acknowledges that he or she has a problem with substance use and plans to take action within the next 6 months or so.

3. *Preparation* is the next stage. Here, the client plans within the next month to take some action regarding the alcohol or drug problem. The client usually lets others know about the change he or she is going to make. Even though the client wants

to change, he or she still has mixed feelings about it: the client does and doesn't want to quit using alcohol or drugs. The client begins to think about the advantages of change.

4. The next stage is *action,* which involves actually changing the alcohol or drug use. The client makes a commitment to stop drinking alcohol, smoking, or using drugs. The commitment could be realized through self-change, a self-help group, or professional treatment. In addition to getting sober or clean, the client begins to learn more about how to change thinking, emotions, self-image, and behavior. The client learns that coping with a substance use problem requires a lot more than simply stopping the use. He or she addresses the "nuts and bolts" issues of recovery such as coping with thoughts and cravings for substances; being aware of people, places, and things that can influence him or her to use again; coping with upsetting feelings; and dealing with family and relationship problems. The client may become involved in self-help groups or other forms of social support and build structure into his or her life to reduce boredom.

5. Relapse prevention is treatment applied during *maintenance,* the next stage of change. During this stage, the client continues to make positive changes in self and lifestyle. The client works to prevent a return to alcohol or drug use and accepts that there are no easy or quick solutions to the substance use problem. The client learns to identify and manage relapse warning signs and high-risk situations. He or she works on balancing the various areas of life to improve self-image. Many people stay in this stage for several years and find it helpful to participate in ongoing recovery programs that help them maintain vigilance about relapse warning signs. This is why it isn't unusual for some people to attend support groups like AA or NA throughout their lives.

6. The final stage of change is called *termination.* In this stage, the substance use problem no longer presents a temptation or threat. The client's previous behavior doesn't return, and he or she has the confidence and skills to cope with life problems so that relapse is not very likely.

Recovery is seldom a smooth or linear process; clients may move back and forth between stages as their condition changes. Clients may revisit issues from early stages while dealing with issues in a later stage of recovery. For example, a client who has been abstinent for a significant period, is well-grounded in recovery, and is working on changing interpersonal style to have more satisfying relationships could temporarily experience strong cravings and pressures to drink alcohol. Another client may have a lapse or relapse, requiring that the focus shift to reestablishing abstinence.

Objectives of the Session

1. To introduce the client to the concept of stages of change

2. To help the client identify his or her current stage of change and issues to address in recovery

3. To review strategies to help the client deal with low motivation

4. To identify therapy-sabotaging behaviors and positive coping strategies

Major Points and Issues for Discussion

1. The therapist should discuss the concept of stages of change and help the client become aware that recovery is not a linear process in which he or she moves smoothly from one stage to the next; the stages are general guidelines to help the client know what to expect during the recovery process. The time a client spends in a specific recovery stage is highly individual and depends on his or her unique situation, motivation to change, social supports, and capability to change.

2. The therapist should help the client determine which stage of recovery he or she is in by having the client complete the Assessing Your Stage of Change Worksheet (see Chapter 5 in the Client Workbook).

3. The therapist can help clients address motivational struggles during recovery by using any of the following strategies.

   The client can review the reasons for quitting substance use and identify short-term and long-term benefits. The client should complete the Decision-Making Matrix (see Figure 7.1 in this guide and Chapter 5 in the Client Workbook), which lists short-term and long-term consequences (positive and negative) of stopping or continuing substance use.

Decision-Making Matrix
Pros and cons of quitting

Instructions: In the sections below, write the pros and cons of quitting and of continuing to use alcohol, tobacco, or other drugs. Provide examples of both immediate and long-term consequences of each decision.

	Immediate consequences		Long-term consequences	
	Positive	**Negative**	**Positive**	**Negative**
To stop using or remain abstinent	Better sleep Fewer family arguments Save money No hangovers Won't feel guilty	Bored Cravings are strong Hard to be around drinking buddies Frustration Denial of pleasure	Better health Happier family life Won't lose job Much better financial condition	Need to have new fun activities

	Immediate consequences		Long-term consequences	
	Positive	**Negative**	**Positive**	**Negative**
To continue using	Relaxes me It's familiar Fit in with friends	Wife upset Costs a lot Lost time at work Feel guilty	Always an easy way to escape reality or unpleasant feelings	Health problems Could lose job Family frustration with me will increase Could lose family and friends Hate myself

Figure 7.1.   Example of Completed Decision-Making Matrix

The client can review the problems caused or worsened by substance use and identify problems that might occur if he or she continues to use alcohol or other drugs. The client should review his or her completed Harmful Effects Worksheet (see Figure 3.1 in Chapter 3 of this guide and Chapter 3 in the Client Workbook), in which he or she identified problems in functioning that are associated with the substance use.

The client can think about specific adverse effects of substance use on important people such as family members (e.g., spouse, children).

The client can remind himself or herself that motivational crises usually pass in time and that sticking with the recovery program is the best way to lower relapse potential.

The client can seek help or guidance from the therapist, peers in recovery, or supportive friends and family.

The client can pray or meditate.

Some clients will need help in facing their reluctance to examine ways in which their substance use problem adversely affects others. Clients involved in a 12-step program can be encouraged to learn about the "making amends" steps (steps 8 and 9) that can help them undo some of the damage caused to others. Clients who specifically attempt to make amends should be prepared for the possibility that other people may not respond favorably. Clients sometimes experience anger, hostility, and rejection when they attempt to make amends with a family member, friend, or colleague. The client who anticipates and prepares for others' adverse reactions will be better able to cope should these actually occur. This preparation may require changing negative interpretations of rejection or anger so that it is not taken personally. Some interpersonal relationships will have been harmed so much that the client's attempts to make amends will never be accepted.

4. The therapist should introduce the client to therapy-sabotaging behaviors. These are attitudes and behaviors that decrease the likelihood of positive change or appropriate use of therapy. A few examples are (a) not attending therapy sessions on time or missing them; (b) not following through and completing recovery assignments or journal exercises between therapy sessions; and (c) not opening up and sharing thoughts, feelings, or problems with the therapist. If a client has previously participated in treatment, the therapist should have him

or her complete the Therapy-Sabotaging Behavior Worksheet (see Figure 7.2 in this guide and Chapter 6 in the Client Workbook). The therapist and client can use the client's answers to collaboratively develop strategies to minimize and cope with such behaviors should they occur in the future.

As the client progresses through recovery and establishes a foundation of abstinence, he or she will become more able to face emotional issues from the past, examine personality issues (often referred to as "character defects" in 12-step programs), and focus on broader issues such as how and why to work toward a balanced lifestyle.

In all stages of recovery, clients face the possibility of lapse and relapse. Any lapse or relapse should be discussed with the therapist, and can also be discussed with members of the client's recovery support system.

Therapy-Sabotaging Behavior Worksheet

Instructions: Review each behavior below. Place a check mark (✓) next to it if you've ever experienced it in relation to your therapy or counseling. Then, choose two behaviors you have experienced and develop an action plan for coping with each behavior.

✓ Not attending my sessions on time

_____ Skipping my session entirely

_____ Missing sessions because I was upset with my counselor

_____ Dropping out of counseling after only a few sessions

✓ Not following through and completing assignments or journal exercises between my counseling sessions

_____ Blaming my counselor for not helping me enough

_____ Talking about how to change in my sessions but not actually translating these changes into my life

_____ Expecting my counselor to solve my problems

_____ Expecting my counselor to tell me what to talk about in my sessions

_____ Not opening up and telling my counselor what I really think or feel

_____ Not telling my counselor when I feel like using substances or have actually used between sessions

_____ Constantly calling my counselor on the phone or leaving messages

_____ Placing unrealistic demands on my counselor

_____ Not properly taking medications such as Antabuse® or naltrexone, or medications for a concurrent psychiatric disorder

_____ Not accepting responsibility for those things over which I have control

_____ Not accepting responsibility for _____ (things over which I have influence)

_____ Blaming others for my behavior choices

_____ Placing myself in high-risk situations

Behavior 1: _Not attending sessions on time_

Action Plan: _Figure out why I'm late for my sessions and other things in my life; think about my sessions as being scheduled a half-hour before the actual time; remind myself that I'm the one who misses out if I get less time for counseling; and make an agreement with my therapist that I will show up on time._

Behavior 2: _Not following through and completing the assignments or journal exercises between my counseling sessions._

Action Plan: _Both this problem and the one above seem to relate to my problem of being responsible. I've got to change my attitude and constantly tell myself that doing what I'm supposed to do is for my own good; challenge my poor excuses that I "forget" to do my assignments; and set time aside each week to carefully review and complete my assignment._

Figure 7.2. **Example of Completed Therapy-Sabotaging Behavior Worksheet**

Chapter 8

Session Topic: Goal Planning in Recovery

Note: This session covers Chapter 7 in the Client Workbook.

Introduction

Recovery can be viewed as a process that addresses any major domain of the client's functioning: physical, emotional or psychological, family, social or interpersonal, spiritual, or lifestyle. The goals a particular client chooses and his or her ability to meet these goals depend on the client's stage of recovery as well as several other factors:

■ severity of the substance use and problems caused by it

■ motivation to change

■ internal psychological resources (e.g., insight, resilience, capacity for tolerating distress, ability to work toward long-term goals and delay gratification)

■ interpersonal relationships and external support system

Recovery involves making changes and developing specific skills to deal with the problems and demands of being substance-free. Following is a review of some of the changes that clients may wish to make in each major domain of functioning.

■ *Physical.* Take care of medical or dental problems, improve diet, lose weight, practice stress reduction, exercise, and learn to cope with physical cravings to use substances.

■ *Emotional or Psychological.* Accept the substance use problem; change negative or distorted thinking or beliefs; improve ability to cope with stress, problems in life, or upsetting feelings; address coexisting psychiatric disorders; and deal with past psychological trauma.

- *Family.* Involve the family in the recovery process, assess the impact of substance use on the family, make amends for harm caused to family, and work with the family to improve communication and interactions.

- *Social or interpersonal.* Establish relationships with sober people; participate in enjoyable leisure activities that don't involve substance use; learn to refuse offers to use substances; address interpersonal conflicts or problems; and deal with legal, financial, work, or academic problems caused by substance use.

- *Spiritual.* Deal with guilt and shame issues, develop meaning in life, and explore other personal aspects of spiritual growth.

Objectives of the Session

1. To help the client learn about the various domains of functioning related to recovery

2. To help the client identify specific recovery goals related to the various domains of functioning

3. To help the client develop strategies to reach his or her identified goals

Major Points and Issues for Discussion

1. The therapist and client should discuss the recovery process and different domains of recovery: physical, emotional or psychological, family, social or interpersonal, spiritual and lifestyle.

2. The therapist and client should discuss the client's main goal in relation to substance use. Although many clients will choose total abstinence as their initial goal, some may choose a reduction in use. For example, not all clients with an alcohol problem will be physically or psychologically dependent on alcohol or suffer numerous adverse effects from drinking. Some of these clients may wish to drink less alcohol so that drinking does not cause any harm in their lives.

The therapist should determine if reduction of substance use is realistic for the client who chooses this goal. If the client has a history of substance dependence, suffers many adverse effects of substance use, has a significant, concurrent medical or psychiatric problem, or may suffer a major loss if substances are used (e.g., clients who are mandated to quit by court or employer), reduction of use is not a realistic goal. The client will ultimately choose the goal that he or she wants over the goal that the therapist wants. However, if the therapist strongly feels that total abstinence is the most appropriate goal, he or she should share this position with the client and give a rationale.

The therapist should help the client prioritize recovery goals and provide feedback regarding the client's goals and proposed strategies to achieve these goals. The client should understand the importance of having both short-term and long-term goals. Goals provide a measuring stick by which progress can be evaluated. The client should complete the Goal Planning Worksheet (see Figure 8.1 in this guide and Chapter 7 in the Client Workbook) to guide him or her in the process of identifying goals and developing an action plan to achieve these goals.

Some clients will have difficulty identifying change issues and setting specific goals. Problem checklists such as the *Substance Abuse Problem Checklist* (Carroll, 1984) or recovery workbooks can help them with this process.

3. It is generally preferable for the therapist to move the client toward finding his or her own strategies for dealing with a specific problem or recovery issue. However, the therapist can provide additional suggestions when appropriate. It is helpful in the early stages of recovery for the therapist to give direct suggestions, especially when the client is struggling with a particular issue or problem that threatens his or her sobriety such as persistent cravings, periods of low motivation, or pressure from a significant other to use substances.

When working with the client on a specific problem or recovery issue, the therapist should assess the client's coping skills to determine if he or she needs additional help in learning specific skills to manage a particular problem. For example, knowing that a client has inadequate coping skills and is at high risk to act out angry feelings through violence or substance

Goal Planning Worksheet

Instructions: For each domain of recovery, list any changes you want to make. For each change that you identify, write the steps you can take to help you achieve your goal. Try to be as concrete as you can in identifying your goals and your change strategies.

Change:	Goal:	Steps toward change:
Physical	Lose 20 pounds.	Start a regular exercise program; change diet to reduce calories taken in; greatly reduce amount of sweets I eat; don't keep cakes and pies in my house.
Emotional or psychological	Learn to control angry impulses.	Catch myself early when I'm mad so I don't let things build up; learn to put my feelings into words; figure out if things are really worth getting mad about; walk away if I feel like getting physical with someone else.
Family	Gain the trust of my family back. A better relationship with my kids.	Accept that I have to be patient with my family; invite them to attend counseling sessions with me; spend time with my kids; take an active role in their lives by being interested in what they say and do; attend my kids' sports and school events.
Social or interpersonal	Improve relationship with Jason.	Invite him over for dinner; apologize for taking advantage of him when I was drinking and explain that I'm working at sobriety; offer to help him.
Spiritual	Reduce guilty feelings about myself and empty feeling.	Share feelings in therapy and group meetings; pray; return to regular church services.
Other (work, economic, etc.)	Reduce debt and save money for emergencies.	Prioritize my debts; make and follow a budget; have $50 taken out of each paycheck for my savings account.

Figure 8.1. **Example of Completed Goal Planning Worksheet**

use can help the therapist devise interventions to address this specific deficit.

In helping the client to improve or develop new coping skills, the therapist should focus on cognitive, behavioral, and interpersonal strategies so that the client is exposed to a variety of approaches to dealing with problems. For example, improving relationships may require a client to alter beliefs regarding reciprocity or self-disclosure, learn to act more assertively, or learn to be more empathetic toward others.

If the client is unable to meet a particular goal, the therapist should help him or her figure out what is getting in the way. Is the goal too ambitious or unrealistic? Does the client have adequate internal or external resources to help him or her reach the goal? Are there significant people who are sabotaging the client's effort to reach the goal?

Chapter 9

Session Topic: Managing Cravings and Urges to Use Substances

Note: This session covers Chapter 8 in the Client Workbook.

Introduction

A craving or longing for alcohol, tobacco, or other drugs is very common, especially in the early weeks and months of stopping substance use, regardless of how motivated clients are to stay substance-free. Cravings are mediated by brain activation in the amygdala region. Cravings can be activated by exposure to drug cues via classical conditioning. An urge is the client's intention to use alcohol or drugs once he or she experiences a craving. Usually, cravings decrease in frequency and intensity as recovery progresses and the client abstains from substance use. The client may be surprised by how strong a craving can be and how it can increase positive thoughts about the effects of a substance. The client who is overcoming a physical addiction is especially vulnerable to cravings during the first days and weeks of abstinence. Some clients report an overwhelming compulsion to use substances when they first stop using, even after completing the acute withdrawal process, a condition influenced by changes in brain neurochemistry, psychological coping mechanisms, and the social environment.

External factors trigger cravings. External factors include people with whom the client associated while drinking or using drugs; places or events where substances were used; and situations in which alcohol, tobacco, or other drugs were available. Many environmental cues trigger cravings: food; coffee; the sight or smell of alcohol or drugs; ads for liquor or tobacco products; cigarette machines; tobacco shops; driving by a bar or club where the client used to drink; needles, mirrors, pipes, papers, or other drug paraphernalia; and music associated with partying, money, paychecks, or sex. The list of environmental cues is endless. In addition to common ones mentioned above, there are many cues unique to each person in recovery.

Internal factors trigger cravings as well. Internal factors include feelings such as anger, anxiety, boredom, depression, or frustration; physical pain or symptoms; and positive memories or thoughts of using substances. Physical withdrawal symptoms are very powerful triggers during the early stages of stopping substance use.

The intensity of a craving can vary from mild to extremely strong and powerful. Some clients report feeling overwhelmed and tortured by cravings when they first initiate recovery. It takes time for their bodies to adjust to being substance-free and for them to learn practical ways of managing cravings. The risk of relapse increases for clients who are unable to identify cravings and implement coping strategies.

Objectives of the Session

1. To help the client define and label a craving to use substances

2. To teach the client to monitor and track cravings over time, and to rate the level of intensity of cravings

3. To identify internal and external factors that trigger cravings

4. To help the client learn cognitive, behavioral, environmental, and interpersonal strategies to manage cravings.

Major Points and Issues for Discussion

1. The therapist should teach the client to identify cravings as the first step to managing them. The client needs to know how cravings show in physical and mental symptoms and behaviors. Cravings show in anxiety; restlessness; stomach distress; excessive energy; inability to sit still; irritability; or thoughts, fantasies, and dreams of using. They may be overt so that the client is aware of them, or they may be covert and out of the client's immediate awareness.

   The therapist should inform the client that cravings to use alcohol, tobacco, or other drugs are very common after one stops using, especially in the first few weeks or months of recovery. Cravings can be experienced regardless of how motivated a client is to stay substance-free; therefore, being able to identify and label cravings is necessary for recovery to progress.

2. The client should complete the Daily Craving Record (see Figure 9.1 in this guide and Chapter 8 in the Client Workbook) for several weeks or months to monitor and rate cravings during the early phases of recovery. Daily ratings help the client to remain vigilant and to see how cravings wax and wane over time. The severity of cravings often declines as recovery progresses. Certain patterns may emerge as the client rates cravings regularly. For example, a client may become aware that cravings are more intense during certain times or days of the week. As shown in Figure 9.1, Sharon's daily ratings were severe for the first 2 to 3 weeks and moderate to severe during the next 2 to 3 weeks. The intensity of her cravings decreased during months 2 and 3. About 6 weeks into her abstinence (November 16th), she experienced severe cravings for a day. Recently, her cravings have increased. Sharon has been able to identify a connection between upset feelings in a relationship and an increase in severity of cravings.

   Identifying the client's weakest and strongest periods of cravings and urges since the last session and processing what was different between the weakest and strongest periods can help the client learn what contributes to more difficult periods. This in turn can lead to discussions on how to manage times during which cravings and urges are the strongest and the client feels most vulnerable.

   Cravings can take on a life of their own and exert a great influence on the client's thinking and actions. For example, reactions to an intense craving can lead to relapse if the client goes into a bar to socialize or attends a party where drugs are readily available.

3. The therapist should emphasize the importance of identifying both external and internal factors that trigger cravings. The should client complete the Substance Use Triggers Worksheet (see Figure 9.2 in this guide and Chapter 8 in the Client Workbook). This worksheet can be used to identify external triggers such as people, places, events, or situations that directly or indirectly affect the client's desire to use substances. The worksheet can also be used to identify internal triggers such as thoughts, feelings, memories, times of day, fantasies, dreams, and physical sensations. The client should look for not only

Ratings of Intensity of Cravings

Instructions: Each day, use the scale to rate the average intensity (0–5) of your cravings to use alcohol, tobacco, or other drugs.

0	1	2	3	4	5
None	Low		Moderate		Severe

Month: October

Day	1	2	3	4	5	6	7	8	9	10	11	12	13	14	15	16
Rating	5	5	4	4	5	5	4	4	5	4	4	3	4	4	5	4
Day	17	18	19	20	21	22	23	24	25	26	27	28	29	30	31	
Rating	4	3	3	3	4	3	3	5	3	3	3	3	2	3	3	

Month: November

Day	1	2	3	4	5	6	7	8	9	10	11	12	13	14	15	16
Rating	3	3	2	4	3	3	3	2	2	3	3	3	3	3	3	5
Day	17	18	19	20	21	22	23	24	25	26	27	28	29	30	31	
Rating	3	2	3	3	3	3	2	2	3	2	3	3	3	3		

Month: December

Day	1	2	3	4	5	6	7	8	9	10	11	12	13	14	15	16
Rating	3	2	2	3	3	2	2	1	2	2	2	2	2	3	2	1
Day	17	18	19	20	21	22	23	24	25	26	27	28	29	30	31	
Rating	1	2	2	1	2	2	2	2	2							

Figure 9.1. **Example of Completed Daily Craving Record**

obvious triggers, but for ones that may be more subtle but just as influential. The therapist can help the client rate the degree of threat of each trigger and deal first with the highest rated triggers, as these represent the greatest relapse risk.

4. The therapist should review the client's coping strategies to help determine their potential usefulness. The therapist should try to ensure that the client has a variety of strategies to manage cravings and that the strategies discussed are related to the client's situation.

   The therapist should review environmental coping strategies such as (a) reducing environmental cues by getting rid of substances the client is trying to quit; and (b) getting rid of paraphernalia associated with preparing or using substances such as lighters, ashtrays, needles, mirrors, pipes, and papers.

   The therapist should review cognitive coping strategies such as (a) learning to talk oneself out of using when one craves alcohol, tobacco, or other drugs; (b) reminding oneself that cravings are temporary and will pass in time; (c) putting off responding to the craving for awhile in order to buy time; (d) remembering the negative aspects of substance use and the positive aspects of not using; (e) reminding oneself that cravings are usually triggered by external cues, *not* by willpower failure, and that just because one experiences a craving does not mean that one has to give in to the urge—one can accept craving as a natural conditioning reaction; and (f) meditating or asking for help through prayer or personal dialogue with God or a higher power.

   The therapist should review behavioral coping strategies such as (a) avoiding or escaping high-risk situations and finding alternative activities, (b) distracting oneself through involvement in an activity unrelated to substance use, (c) engaging in physical exercise or activities to release tension, (d) writing in a journal or filling in the Daily Craving Record, and (e) reading recovery literature for information or inspiration.

   The therapist should review interpersonal coping strategies such as (a) talking to other people in recovery and (b) talking to friends or family members.

   The therapist should also review pharmacologic strategies that may help to ameliorate cravings for specific substances. Specific medications are discussed in Chapter 6.

Substance-Use Triggers Worksheet

Instructions: List people, places, events, situations, objects, feelings, thoughts, memories, or times of day that trigger your cravings or urges. Rate the level of threat presented by each trigger using the scale below. Finally, list strategies for coping with each trigger that will help you avoid using.

0	1	2	3	4	5
No Threat			Moderate Threat		Severe Threat

Trigger (external or internal)	Level of threat (0–5)	Coping strategies
Drug dealer	5	Avoid him; don't talk on phone when he calls.
Guys I got high with	5	Stop going to parties or socializing where drugs are used; limit contact to non-drug use activities; avoid some guys completely.
Brother and his apartment	3	Let him know I quit using and ask him not to offer me drugs or use around me; have visits with him at my place.
Angry after arguing with girlfriend	4	Stop using this as an excuse to get high; learn to accept that it's OK to get mad without using for revenge or to "show her."
Feeling bored	4	Accept that my boredom will pass; have a list of activities to keep me occupied when boredom gets the best of me; take up some new hobbies; remind myself I can have fun without using drugs or being with others at parties who are getting high.
Pipes, mirrors	3	Get rid of my drug paraphernalia.

Figure 9.2. **Examples of Completed Substance Use Triggers Worksheets**

Substance-Use Triggers Worksheet

Instructions: List people, places, events, situations, objects, feelings, thoughts, memories, or times of day that trigger your cravings or urges. Rate the level of threat presented by each trigger using the scale below. Finally, list strategies for coping with each trigger that will help you avoid using.

0	1	2	3	4	5
No Threat			Moderate Threat		Severe Threat

Trigger (external or internal)	Level of threat (0–5)	Coping strategies
Feeling tense and stressed out	4	Practice relaxation techniques; go for walks every day to reduce stress; tell myself I can decompress without a drink or a cigarette.
Coffee in the morning and after dinner	5	Review my reasons for quitting tobacco each morning; pray for strength to not smoke; use dessert coffees after dinner as the desire to smoke is not as great; go for walk with husband after dinner.
Break time at work	4	Change my routine at work during breaks and spend time with the non-smokers; replace cigarettes with gum and mints; and read a magazine during break.
Cocktail hour after work	3	Avoid going to bars after work; have non-alcohol drinks at home after work; ask husband not to drink alcohol in front of me and to have discussion of how our day went; play soothing music before dinner.
Feeling like I deserve a reward (alcohol) after a hard week of work	4	Find other rewards (buy self something nice, go to movie, go out to dinner and movie with husband).
Stressful visit with parents, especially when Dad gets drunk	5	Let parents know I won't stay for visits when Dad drinks; ask Mother to visit at our home if Dad refuses to not drink; ask my husband for support and talk about my upset feelings.
Getting stuck in traffic	3	Play tapes of favorite albums; listen to talk radio; refuse to let myself get frustrated; tell myself "I don't need a cigarette to get through traffic."

Figure 9.2. Examples of Completed Substance Use Triggers Worksheets (*continued*)

73

Clients need encouragement and support in learning, practicing, and implementing coping skills. Although many clients learn these skills easily on an intellectual level, they frequently struggle to implement them in their daily lives. This is why regular practice and active use of coping skills is so important.

When the client reports that he or she has been able to cope with cravings, the therapist should provide reinforcement and help identify which specific strategies were used.

It is generally useful to start each therapy session with a "craving check" to determine if the client has experienced any significant cravings between sessions. This procedure is also a reminder for the client to remain vigilant for cravings.

Chapter 10

Session Topic: Managing Thoughts of Using Substances

Note: This session covers Chapter 9 in the Client Workbook.

Introduction

Clients have many different thoughts about using substances. Positive thoughts of using are commonly associated with many other recovery issues discussed in this program such as cravings, social pressures, family and interpersonal conflicts, and upsetting emotional states. Helping the client to become aware of and manage thoughts of using substances reduces the risk of relapse and raises the client's level of self-confidence.

Clients who experience a high-risk relapse situation and have positive thoughts of using are more vulnerable to actually taking a drink or using a drug or tobacco. This is especially true if the client has little confidence in his or her ability to manage thoughts of using.

Some of the more common thoughts that can lead to relapse relate to

■ belief that the abuse problem has been solved (e.g., "I've got it beat, now" or "I'll never use again."),

■ limited use or testing personal control (e.g., "A few won't hurt."),

■ having fun while sober (e.g., "I can't have fun if I don't use."),

■ relaxation (e.g., "I need something to relax" or "I need something to take the edge off."),

■ stress (e.g., "Life is difficult; I need to escape for awhile."),

■ socialization (e.g., "I can't fit in with others if they use and I don't."), or

■ motivation (e.g., "What's the point in staying sober; it doesn't matter.").

Objectives of the Session

1. To help the client become aware of how thoughts of using substances can contribute to relapse

2. To help the client identify common thoughts and "apparently irrelevant decisions" that precede substance use

3. To help the client learn strategies to manage and challenge thoughts of using alcohol, tobacco, or other drugs

Major Points and Issues for Discussion

1. The therapist should discuss the relationship between thoughts, feelings, and behaviors. A client's beliefs and thoughts influence his or her feelings and actions. Cognitive distortions (or faulty ways of thinking) are associated with depression, anxiety, substance abuse, unhappiness, and numerous interpersonal problems. Examples of various cognitive distortions are shown in Table 10.1.

   The therapist should discuss the relationship between thoughts of using and substance use behaviors. Thoughts of using can build up gradually over time or be experienced quickly and intensely.

2. The therapist should discuss the concept of "apparently irrelevant decisions." These are seemingly unimportant decisions that lead clients to rationalize behaviors that could contribute to a relapse set-up. For example, a client who recently quit drinking but keeps alcohol in her house "in case guests drop by" has made a decision that could have a major impact on relapse. A client who quits using cocaine but decides to attend a party "to see old friends" puts his recovery in jeopardy by being in social situations in which he is likely to feel direct or indirect pressure to get high on cocaine.

   The client needs to be aware of strong thoughts of using and discuss these to figure out the context in which they occur. For example, thoughts of using substances may increase following

Table 10.1.   Examples of Cognitive Distortions

Type of error	Example
Personalizing	Thinking all situations and events revolve around oneself: "Everyone was looking at me and wondering why I was there."
Magnifying	Blowing negative events out of proportion: "This is the worst thing that could happen to me."
Minimizing	Glossing over positive factors; overlooking the fact that nothing really bad happened.
Either/or thinking	Not taking into account the full continuum: "Either I'm a loser or a winner."
Taking events out of context	After a successful interview, focusing on one or two tough questions: "I blew the interview."
Jumping to conclusions	Reaching conclusions without all the facts of a situation: "I have a swollen gland. This must be cancer."
Overgeneralizing	Taking one or two experiences and reaching major conclusions that apply to all situations: "I always fail. I fail at everything I ever try."
Self-blame	Blaming the total self rather than specific behaviors that can be changed: "I'm no good."
Magical thinking	"Everything is bad because of my bad past deeds."
Mind reading	"Everyone there thought I was fat and ugly."
Comparing	Comparing oneself with someone else and ignoring all the basic differences: "Regina's figure is better than mine."
Catastrophizing	Putting the worst possible construction on events: "I know something terrible happened."

interpersonal conflicts, upsetting emotions, disappointments, or positive experiences.

When the client discusses strong cravings for substances, close calls, or actual lapses or relapses, the therapist should inquire about what thoughts were experienced prior to and during the particular situation. This will help raise awareness of the role of cognition in emotional reactions and behaviors.

3. Because thoughts of using substances are common, especially during the early weeks and months of recovery, it is important to have strategies to challenge these thoughts. Otherwise, the risk of relapse increases.

The client should complete the Managing Thoughts of Using Worksheet (see Figure 10.1 in this guide and Chapter 9 in the Client Workbook). This worksheet provides common examples of substance-related thoughts and asks the client to identify additional thoughts. The client then devises counterstatements to help manage thoughts of using. This exercise helps the client practice changing common thoughts of using. In the long run, the client needs to be able to challenge other specific thoughts of using when they occur.

To help the client challenge and dispute thoughts of using, the therapist should review the strategies discussed in the previous chapter on coping with cravings, such as (a) reviewing the benefits of not drinking, smoking, or ingesting drugs; (b) thinking about the long-term, positive effects of remaining abstinent versus the short-term, perceived benefits of using; (c) reviewing the adverse effects of previous substance use as a reminder of the potential negative consequences of giving in to thoughts of using; (d) distracting oneself by thinking about something pleasant, fun, or enjoyable such as a past experience, upcoming event, or vacation; and (e) sharing thoughts with others, especially those in recovery who can offer acceptance, support, and advice.

The therapist should teach the client to negotiate with the "inner self" by buying time and putting off the decision to use for several hours or longer. For example, the client may say, "I'll wait until tomorrow to use." Simply buying oneself time is often sufficient to deal with thoughts of using substances.

Managing Thoughts of Using Worksheet

Instructions: Review the list of common thoughts associated with relapse. Add some personal thoughts to the list. Then, list counterstatements and strategies you can use to change the thoughts in order to control them and prevent them from leading to substance use.

Thoughts	Counterstatements
1. I'll never use again, I've got my problem under control.	Never is a long time; even though I'm not drinking, I still have to remain vigilant.
2. A few cigarettes (drinks, lines of cocaine, etc.) won't hurt.	True, a few won't hurt, but my drinking pattern is to overdo it. I never stop at a few, so a few will hurt me. I don't like to, but total sobriety is necessary for me.
3. I can't have fun or excitement if I don't use.	Says who? I have some things that I enjoy, that are fun. The truth is, I don't need to drink to have fun. I have to take responsibility and make sure I build some fun into my daily life.
4. I need something to take the edge off and help me relax.	There are other ways of relaxing. I can take a walk, exercise, listen to music, or read.
5. Life is difficult. I need to escape for a while.	Sure, life is hard sometimes, but not just for me, for a lot of others, too. I can get away from stress for a while without drinking.
6. I can't fit in with others if they use and I don't.	This is only true for problem drinkers. I know people who drink socially, who don't overdo it. They don't care if I drink or not. I don't need to fit in with the heavy drinkers because it's too much pressure.

Figure 10.1. Example of Completed Managing Thoughts of Using Worksheet

Thoughts	Counterstatements
7. What's the point in staying sober? It really doesn't matter.	Who said staying sober was easy? It does matter a lot if I stay sober. My health will be better, I can be a better mother to my daughter. And, I can keep my life on track only if I'm sober.
8. I'm going to test myself to see if I can have just one.	A better way of testing myself is to see if I can have none. If I have one, I will only want more.
9. How can I go out with Leroy if I don't drink?	Leroy doesn't drink too much. I can tell him about my drinking problem. I can enjoy his company without drinking.
10. I'll never get out of debt, I might as well get drunk.	Things were much worse when I was drinking. At least now, I can pay my bills and care for my daughter even if things are tight. There's no excuse for getting drunk now.
11. I could drink and no one would ever know.	I would know and wouldn't be fooling anyone but myself. I can choose not to drink. I will choose not to drink.

Figure 10.1. **Example of Completed Managing Thoughts of Using Worksheet** (*continued*)

Chapter 11

Session Topic: Dealing With Emotions

Note: This session covers Chapter 10 in the Client Workbook.

Introduction

Ineffective responses to negative emotional states are the most common relapse precipitants, and they pose a challenge for the client in recovery. Negative emotional states can be exacerbated by physical withdrawal as well as by life problems, stresses, and interpersonal difficulties. In addition to having an impact on relapse, a negative affect such as anger, depression, anxiety, boredom, loneliness, guilt, or shame causes unhappiness and distress and contributes to interpersonal difficulties. In some instances negative affect is a symptom of a psychiatric disorder.

Clients may use substances to cover up these feelings or to help cope with them. However, the effects of alcohol or other drugs exaggerate feelings and impair judgment. This in turn leads to the client's inappropriately acting on feelings. For example, mild frustration or anger can be expressed as intense hatred, or normal attraction can be expressed as unremitting love.

Clients may have difficulty recognizing their feelings or may blame others for what they feel. Following is a brief listing of difficulties related to upsetting emotions experienced by clients with alcohol or drug problems.

■ *Anger.* Expressing it too freely or in verbally or physically harmful ways; letting it build and avoiding direct expression of it; letting it control behavior; failure to acknowledge anger toward others; inability to let go of angry feelings toward others; excessive anger at self for having a substance use disorder

- *Anxiety.* Fear or worry about one's ability to stick to recovery, or about specific problems in life; fear that leads to avoidant behaviors and adversely affects the client's ability to function or attend recovery group meetings; persistent and disabling anxiety or fear that does not improve with sobriety or worsens with abstinence, and that is symptomatic of a psychiatric disorder

- *Boredom.* Difficulty having fun without planning to use or actually using substances; inability to enjoy experiences in which substances are not available; trouble adjusting to the routine of sobriety; discovering serious boredom with a job or primary relationship upon getting sober

- *Depression.* Feeling sad due to losses caused by the substance use problem; feeling sad and hopeless about serious problems in career, relationships, or some other major aspect of life; having a persistent mood disorder that doesn't appear to improve or actually worsens with continued sobriety

- *Emptiness.* Feeling a void in which little pleasure, satisfaction, or meaning in life is experienced; feeling persistent emptiness that doesn't abate with longer-term sobriety and may be part of a mood or personality disorder; wondering "Is this all there is?" after a period of sobriety of several months or longer

- *Guilt and shame.* Feeling "bad" about one's actions or inactions related to substance use; feeling "bad," defective, or like a failure for having a substance use problem

- *Loneliness.* Feeling lonely after the substance use disorder contributed to failed relationships; inability to establish and maintain close, interpersonal relationships

When clients stop using substances, they often need to learn to manage emotions in new ways. Some clients have to learn to recognize their feelings and give themselves permission to experience them because they are so out of touch with their affective side. Others need to learn self-control and how to tolerate emotional distress without acting in self-destructive or violent ways. Many clients need help in learning to cope with feelings in responsible, productive ways that lead to continued sobriety, better mental health, and improved interpersonal relationships.

Objectives of the Session

1. To identify the role of negative or positive emotions in recovery and relapse

2. To help the client identify high-risk emotional issues (specific feelings or deficits in coping skills) to address in recovery

3. To help the client learn appropriate strategies for managing upsetting feelings

Major Points and Issues for Discussion

1. The therapist should discuss how negative emotional states contribute to relapse, dissatisfaction in life, or problematic relationships. There is also the possibility that positive emotional states (e.g., excitement, celebration, strong sexual passions) may serve as triggers, especially in an interpersonal context. Some clients use substances to dampen or control *any* strong affect, positive or negative. It is important to be able to manage emotions in recovery. Some clients find this especially difficult when they first stop using substances.

2. The client should complete the Emotions Worksheet (see Figure 11.1 in this guide and Chapter 10 in the Client Workbook) to rate the degree of difficulty dealing with anxiety and worry, anger, boredom, depression, emptiness, guilt, shame, and loneliness without relying on substances. This worksheet also helps the client begin to formulate strategies for coping with problematic feelings.

   The therapist should assess the client's general style of dealing with negative affect. Are upsetting feelings denied, avoided, suppressed, acted out in ways harmful to others, or acted out in ways harmful to the client? Which emotional states are likely to influence the client to use alcohol, tobacco, or other drugs? Which cause the most difficulty in other areas of life or lead to significant personal distress? To become more aware of his or her positive and problematic coping styles, the client can use a journal to record and rate the intensity of feelings and to document thoughts contributing to feelings, the context in which they occur, and coping strategies used.

   The therapist should help the client deal with specific problematic emotions. This requires the client to be able to recognize and accept emotional states rather than rationalizing or suppressing them. This also requires the client to be able to identify problems associated with the feelings and his or her normal style of coping. For example, suppressing anger

Emotions Worksheet

Instructions: For each emotion below, rate the degree of difficulty you have dealing with these feelings without using alcohol or drugs. Then, choose the two emotions that present the most difficulty in your recovery and identify strategies for coping with them.

0	1	2	3	4	5
None	Low		Moderate		Severe

Emotion	Degree of difficulty coping with emotion (0–5)
1. Anxiety and worry	2
2. Anger	5
3. Boredom	5
4. Depression	3
5. Feeling empty—like nothing matters	3
6. Guilt	4
7. Shame	3
8. Loneliness	3

Feeling or emotion	Coping strategies
Boredom	Plan weekends in advance to limit free time on my hands; build in pleasurable activities every single week; accept some boredom as normal and inevitable; tell myself this is a chance to try something new.
Anger	Don't let little things get me so worked up; think things through when I'm angry before I act on them; keep my voice normal when talking to my wife about my anger; remind myself that I can stay in control when angry.

Figure 11.1. **Example of Completed Emotions Worksheet**

and expressing it through passive-aggressive behaviors often leads to interpersonal conflict and dissatisfaction. If a husband is angry at his wife and unable to express it directly, he may express it indirectly. He may "forget" important dates such as his wife's birthday or their anniversary, which can lead to ill feelings and marital strife.

The therapist should help the client figure out what may be contributing to the occurrence of a particular emotional state so that problems can be solved. For example, if a client is depressed due to severe interpersonal conflict associated with an abusive relationship, the relationship may have to be changed so the client can improve the depressed mood. If a client is lonely and disconnected from other people because he or she becomes too dependent in relationships and drives others away with his or her insatiable needs, this pattern will need to be changed so the client can develop appropriate relationships that are mutually beneficial.

3. The therapist should help the client examine and change faulty beliefs and thoughts that may contribute to a specific emotional conflict. For example, thoughts associated with anger, such as "It's bad to get angry" and "If I get angry, I'll lose it and hurt someone" can be changed to "It's normal to get angry; everyone feels this at times" or "I can get angry without losing control and getting violent." Thoughts associated with boredom, such as "I always have to be doing something," "I won't be able to entertain myself," and "Life can't be any fun without substances" can be changed to "I don't need action all the time; it's OK to slow down," "I'm fully capable of finding ways to entertain and enjoy myself," "I can have fun without alcohol or other drugs," or "What evidence is there that a person like me can't have fun without using?" Thoughts associated with depression, such as "It would be terrible if others didn't accept or like me," "I can't make mistakes," and "The worst possible thing is going to happen" can be changed to "There's no way everyone is going to accept or like me; it's just part of life," "Mistakes are normal, so why make a big deal out of any mistakes that I make," and "What evidence do I have that the worst thing is always going to happen?"

The therapist should encourage the client to express feelings directly to others when appropriate or share them with a trusted friend. Learning to disclose feelings is difficult for many clients. Some will need help in learning to talk with others about their feelings. In some instances, clients need to learn assertiveness so they can stand up for themselves and deal with anger, frustration, disappointment, and conflict with another person.

The client should increase structure in daily life. Too much free time, particularly when coupled with a lack of goals, is a high-risk situation for many substance users. Structure can reduce anxiety, boredom, and depression, especially when pleasant activities are included.

The therapist should encourage the client to regularly participate in physical, social, and creative activities. These activities can help reduce stress and release tension and other feelings.

The therapist should encourage the client to read about emotional issues by providing specific recommendations of books or recovery guides. Many informative, inspirational, and hopeful materials are available on virtually any area of emotional difficulty.

The client can also use "inner directed" activities such as meditation or prayer. Such activities can reduce negative feelings, increase energy, and improve the client's outlook on life.

The therapist should consider a medication evaluation for serious negative emotional states (e.g., depression, anxiety) that persist despite the client's using some of the previously discussed strategies. Many clients with substance use problems experience a mood or anxiety disorder at some point in their lives. In some instances, the disorder is severe enough to cause immense personal distress and difficulty functioning. In addition to therapy, non-addictive medications can be quite helpful in treating such disorders. Self-help groups for psychiatric disorders can also help the client gain social support and learn additional strategies for coping with feelings.

Although many clients struggle with negative affect, the therapist should discuss the importance of positive emotional states. For example, helping clients increase their ability to appropriately share positive feelings (e.g., love) often makes them feel better and improves their interpersonal relationships. Discussion should not focus solely on negative affect.

Chapter 12

Session Topic: Refusing Offers to Use Substances

Note: This session covers Chapter 11 in the Client Workbook.

Introduction

One of the most common challenges for any client giving up alcohol, tobacco, or other drugs is resisting social pressures to use substances. According to research studies, social pressures are the second most common relapse precipitant. Clients who are not prepared to resist pressures to use are more vulnerable to relapse.

Direct social pressures include situations in which others offer the client substances. Pressure may vary from mild to extreme, in which another person tries very hard to influence the client to use. The client may feel awkward and very tempted to use. In some social interactions, the possibility of a sexual encounter may be intertwined with alcohol or other drug use (e.g., cocaine or marijuana), adding to the pressure felt to use substances.

The client is also likely to experience indirect social pressure during situations in which alcohol, tobacco, or other drugs are being used but no one is directly pressuring the client to use substances. The desire to use can be very high in such situations. For example, a person who gives up alcohol and attends a work-related social function where others are drinking can feel very tempted. A person who has given up smoking can be at a party or in a restaurant where others are smoking and feel pressure to smoke.

Because avoiding all people who use substances and events and situations in which others may be using substances is not possible, the client needs to prepare to resist any social pressure he or she encounters. Preparing ahead of time can make the client feel more comfortable and confident when handling various direct and indirect social pressures to use substances.

Objectives of the Session

1. To help the client identify direct and indirect social pressures (people, places, events, social and work situations) to use alcohol, tobacco, or other drugs

2. To identify feelings experienced during social pressure situations (e.g., anger, anxiety, excitement)

3. To identify thoughts experienced during social pressure situations (e.g., wanting to fit in, wanting to be normal)

4. To identify strategies to avoid high-risk people, places, situations, and events and to cope with social pressures that cannot be avoided

Major Points and Issues for Discussion

1. The therapist should discuss how social pressures, both direct and indirect, affect relapse, and should emphasize the importance of identifying social pressures and having strategies to avoid or resist them.

The client should complete the Social Pressures Worksheet (see Figure 12.1 in this guide and Chapter 11 in the Client Workbook) to identify specific people who might pressure the client and places, events, and situations in which social pressures are likely to be experienced. The therapist can use the client's difficulty rating for each social pressure to prioritize those that represent the greatest or most immediate relapse risk.

The therapist should have the client identify which pressures represent the greatest challenge to recovery, and ascertain the client's level of confidence in successfully resisting these pressures to use. (For example, a client who worries she will not fit in with peers who drink, or who thinks she can't have any fun if others drink, is likely to experience strong pressures to use alcohol.) A client who anticipates, prepares for, and feels

Social Pressures Worksheet

Instructions: List specific direct or indirect social pressures to use alcohol, tobacco, or other drugs that you expect to face. For each social pressure you list, use the scale below to rate the degree of difficulty you believe you will have coping successfully with that pressure. Finally, list coping strategies you can use to cope with these social pressures.

0	1	2	3	4	5
No Threat			Moderate Threat		Severe Threat

Social pressures	Degree of difficulty (0–5)	Coping strategies
Mark (brother)	4	Don't go to bars or clubs. Tell Mark, Sam, and Jack I'm not drinking anymore
Sam (brother-in-law)	5	and ask them not to pressure me to have a few. Leave after softball games
Jack (drinking buddy)	4	instead of staying around and drinking. Leave Mark's garage if the guys drink.
		Stop monthly poker games until I feel like I can handle them.
Ballpark	3	Plan non-drinking activities for picnics. Tell myself I can have a good time
Brother's garage	4	without drinking.
Red's Bar & Grill	5	
Family picnics	4	Develop new hobbies that don't involve drinking. Attend social events at local
Get-togethers at Mike's house	4	recovery club.
Annual work Christmas party	5	
Monthly poker games	4	

Figure 12.1.   Examples of Completed Social Pressures Worksheets

Social Pressures Worksheet

Instructions: List specific direct or indirect social pressures to use alcohol, tobacco, or other drugs that you expect to face. For each social pressure you list, use the scale below to rate the degree of difficulty you believe you will have coping successfully with that pressure. Finally, list coping strategies you can use to cope with these social pressures.

0	1	2	3	4	5
No Threat			Moderate Threat		Severe Threat

Social pressures	Degree of difficulty (0–5)	Coping strategies
Husband	4	Ask husband not to smoke in front of me at home. Request smokers to smoke
Smokers at work	5	outside when visiting my house.
Friends who smoke	4	
Home	4	Spend more time with non-smoking friends. Change habits at work to avoid
Any friend's home	4	smoking at coffee breaks or after lunch. Request non-smoking section at
Restaurants	3	restaurants and ask husband for his support.
Dinner out	3	Have gum or mints with me when at someone else's home who smokes.
Break time at work	3/4	
Socializing with friends who smoke	4	
Morning coffee or dinner at home	5	
with husband		

Figure 12.1. Examples of Completed Social Pressures Worksheets (*continued*)

confident that she has the skills to cope with social pressures has a greater chance of successfully coping with these pressures.

The therapist and client should explore the nuances of social pressure situations to see if there is more going on than meets the eye. For example, it isn't uncommon for some clients to put their recovery at risk for the opportunity to experience a sexual encounter. Some clients minimize or deny the risks associated with such interpersonal interactions. Also, some clients experience relapse set-ups by putting themselves in situations in which they are likely to be pressured to use substances. For example, a client with an alcohol problem who is fairly new to recovery and who goes to the local club to socialize with drinking buddies with the intention of drinking "only soda" raises his vulnerability to drinking. The same holds true for the ex-smoker who joins colleagues at work during their smoking break.

Some clients will be involved in a social network comprised mainly of active substance users, involved in a primary relationship (spouse, partner, roommate) with a substance user, or work in a situation where substances are used or abused. The client will need to carefully evaluate these situations in order to determine how to cope with them. These situations represent a major threat to many clients and often require significant changes.

2. The therapist should help the client become aware of feelings generated by social pressures. Feelings may range from excitement and positive anticipation to anxiety or dread. In early recovery, the client is likely to feel ambivalent: on the one hand, he or she would like to give in to pressures to use; on the other hand, he or she would like to remain sober.

3. The therapist should help the client become aware of thoughts generated by social pressures, such as "I can't fit in unless I use" or "What's the big deal about a few drinks or cigarettes?" Then, the therapist can help the client change his or her specific thoughts. Thoughts and feelings generated by social pressures determine what a client does to cope.

4. The therapist should discuss the importance of avoiding certain high-risk people, places, events, and situations as a relapse prevention strategy. For example, bars, parties in which alcohol is used excessively or drugs are available, and socializing

with active substance abusers or addicts are common high-risk situations that can usually be avoided.

Many clients benefit from behavioral rehearsals or role-plays in which they practice specific ways of assertively refusing offers to use substances. The therapist can help the client use different words, tones of voice, and body language in order to feel confident to resist pressures to use.

Clients can offset the potential impact of social influences on relapse by eliciting support from a recovery treatment group, self-help group, or friend or family member (see Chapter 14 for a review of recovery support systems).

Chapter 13

Session Topic: Dealing With Family and Interpersonal Problems

Note: This session covers Chapter 12 in the Client Workbook.

Introduction

Family and interpersonal problems are common in recovery. Research shows that interpersonal conflict is the third most common relapse risk factor among alcoholics, smokers, and heroin addicts (Daley & Marlatt, 1992). Addressing family and interpersonal issues facilitates the recovery process, helps reverse some of the damage caused during the active phase of substance use, and increases satisfaction with relationships. Clients who fail to address family and interpersonal problems set themselves up to feel angry, frustrated, and unhappy, and raise their risk of relapse.

Helpful clinical interventions include reviewing the effects of substance use problems on family and social relationships, eliciting and listening to the experiences of family members, identifying specific interpersonal problems and concerns, and identifying deficits in interpersonal style. These interventions can improve the client's interpersonal effectiveness, thus reducing the risk of relapse.

Objectives of the Session

1. To identify specific effects of the substance use problem on family and interpersonal relationships

2. To help the client identify specific strategies to cope with family and interpersonal problems caused by the substance use

3. To help the client improve interpersonal effectiveness

Major Points and Issues for Discussion

1. The therapist should discuss how substance use problems affect the family. The client should complete the Family Effects Worksheet (see Figure 13.1 in this guide and Chapter 12 in the Client Workbook). This worksheet has the client identify specific family members adversely affected by the client's substance use. The client also provides examples of problem behaviors and their impact on the family. This worksheet helps the client personalize the information covered in therapy.

   When reviewing this worksheet with the client, the therapist should ask for more details when appropriate. For example, if a client reported missing important events in the life of his child, the therapist would ask for specific examples such as birthdays or graduations. How does the client feel about the relationship being discussed and about having hurt the family member? Clients may feel guilty and ashamed, and some may deny or minimize the adverse effects of their substance use on their family, especially on their children. The therapist can help the client understand the family's experience by inquiring about what it was like for a specific family member to be exposed to the client's substance use and related behaviors.

   If the client is involved in a 12-step program such as AA or NA, the therapist can discuss the effects on the family in the context of steps 8 and 9 (the "making amends" steps).

   The therapist should also discuss how the client's substance use affected other interpersonal relationships. The client should complete the Relationships Worksheet (see Figure 13.2 in this guide and Chapter 12 in the Client Workbook). This worksheet helps the client identify specific interpersonal problems and formulate strategies for improving them.

   The therapist should help the client prioritize interpersonal problems so he or she can deal first with the greatest threats to recovery. Common relationship problems that interfere with recovery include involvement with family members, a partner, or friends who are active substance abusers; lack of healthy or supportive relationships; involvement in abusive or non-reciprocal relationships; and involvement in relationships characterized by chronic chaos or criticism.

   When exploring specific interpersonal relationship problems, the therapist should help the client view the reciprocal nature

Family Effects Worksheet

Instructions: List your family members. Then, describe ways in which the behaviors related to your substance use problem have affected each family member.

Family member	Behaviors/consequences of my substance use
Parents	Borrowed money and never paid it back; stole checks and forged them; never took an interest in parents; used them to bail me out of trouble; upset and worried them, and caused them to be distrustful toward me.
Wife	Lied to her; ignored her; used family income to buy drugs; sold some of her jewelry; she became so distressed and hurt, she left me.
Son	Missed many important events when he was small; didn't spend enough time with him; hard on him when my wife and I separated because of my drug problem.
Brother	Sometimes, I didn't show up for work when I was supposed to help him; created excuses and lies to cover my tracks; disappointed him; he knew I was having drug problems and worried about me.

Figure 13.1. Example of Completed Family Effects Worksheet

Relationships Worksheet

Instructions: Describe the problematic relationships in your life. Write about what you can do to improve these relationships.

Problem	Ways to improve problem
I get too easily angry at my son helping him with homework.	Keep in mind he's only in fourth grade and remind myself to be more patient; take a break if I feel too upset with him until I cool off; give him positive feedback when his work is neat and done correctly; and ask my husband to help our son during times in which I feel too stressed out.
Tension between me and my older sister.	Invite her over for lunch; bring up my concerns and engage her in discussion to figure out how we can get our relationship back on track.
Don't get out alone with husband enough.	Stop making excuses that we are too busy and regularly plan fun activities; let him know I want more alone time with him, that it's important to me; plan a surprise date with him.

Figure 13.2. **Example of Completed Relationships Worksheet**

of relationships and his or her role in these problems. Clients often blame relationship problems on the other person and deny or minimize responsibility for their own roles.

2. The therapist should ask the client what steps can be taken to begin dealing with the adverse impact that his or her substance use problem has had on family members. Both general strategies (e.g., inviting family members to attend counseling sessions or self-help meetings, providing educational materials to the family) and specific strategies (e.g., concrete ways of improving a specific relationship with a child or spouse) should be discussed.

   The client should have open discussions with family members regarding the substance use problem and change plan. If the client is too worried or feels unable to do this, the therapist can ask the client to bring the family to sessions to discuss these issues. The client needs to understand that family members may have some reactions and feelings that may be difficult to hear.

   The therapist should discuss the potential risks and benefits of inviting the client's family to become involved in the recovery process. Some family members will be helpful and supportive, but others may be angry, hostile, and resistant to supporting the recovering member in this way.

   The therapist can invite the family to individual or group sessions to help them learn about substance use problems and the recovery process, and to provide them with an opportunity to talk about their experiences, questions, and concerns.

   The therapist can encourage the client to invite family members to appropriate family support groups such as Alanon, Naranon, Alateen, or Adult Children of Alcoholics (ACOA). The therapist can also directly invite the family to attend such meetings.

   The therapist should determine if there are any serious problems in the family that might require further evaluations, treatment, or both. The therapist should then facilitate any evaluations or treatment needed, if appropriate. For example, if a client reported that a teenage daughter was very depressed and suicidal, and was not receiving any type of mental health care, the therapist would help the client arrange for an evaluation of the daughter.

3. Clients who are farther along in recovery, with substantial sober time, can benefit from exploring and changing their interpersonal behaviors. Such clients should complete the Interpersonal Style Worksheet (see Figure 13.3 in this guide and Chapter 12

Instructions: Following is a list of statements about interpersonal style. In the second column, circle the number that corresponds to the extent to which each statement describes you. Then complete the two items below the list of statements.

	Doesn't describe me		Somewhat describes me			Definitely describes me
1. I say what I think or feel to others and don't hold anything back.	0	1	2	3	4	(5)
2. I worry about hurting others and hold on to my feelings.	(0)	1	2	3	4	5
3. I lash out at others when I'm upset or mad at them.	0	1	2	3	(4)	5
4. I regularly share positive feelings with others.	0	1	2	3	(4)	5
5. I often criticize others a lot and express negative feelings.	0	1	2	3	4	(5)
6. I have trouble talking to strangers.	0	1	(2)	3	4	5
7. I consider myself to be shy and have trouble opening up to others.	0	(1)	2	3	4	5
8. I relate easily to others and like meeting new people.	0	1	(2)	3	4	5
9. I let other people close to me know what's important to me.	0	1	2	3	(4)	5
10. I don't like to argue with others and avoid arguments when I can.	0	1	(2)	3	4	5
11. I let people take advantage of me too easily.	(0)	1	2	3	4	5
12. I consider myself to be an aggressive person.	0	1	2	3	4	(5)
13. I consider myself to be an assertive person.	0	1	2	3	4	(5)
14. I consider myself to be a pushover and a passive person.	(0)	1	2	3	4	5
15. I avoid situations where I have to talk in front of other people.	0	1	(2)	3	4	5
16. I use alcohol, tobacco, or other drugs to help me socialize with others.	0	1	(2)	3	4	5

Identify one aspect of your interpersonal style that you want to change.

I often criticize others and express negative feelings.

List several steps you can take to help you change this behavior.

I'm most critical of my wife and kids, so I'll start by not yelling at them in a nasty voice; I'll think about why I'm feeling negative toward them and be more realistic about what I expect; I'll also consciously make efforts to say something positive to my wife and kids every day, so that I'm not always focused on the negative.

Figure 13.3. **Example of Completed Interpersonal Style Worksheet**

in the Client Workbook). This worksheet will help identify the client's interpersonal strengths as well as aspects of interpersonal style that play a role in relationship problems.

After problems related to interpersonal style have been identified, the therapist can help the client begin to examine and change interpersonal deficits. For example, if a client identified shyness or lack of assertiveness as an interpersonal problem, the client and therapist would explore specific ways in which these problems could be addressed. Behavioral rehearsals are often effective in helping clients begin to develop more effective communication or assertiveness skills. Cognitive interventions are often effective in getting clients to change their beliefs about how they should communicate and behave in their relationships.

Chapter 14

Session Topic: Building a Recovery Support System

Note: This session covers Chapter 13 in the Client Workbook.

Introduction

A positive social support system is associated with better outcome for clients who are overcoming alcohol or drug problems. Healthy and supportive relationships with family, friends, and other recovering individuals offer many potential benefits. The pressure to use substances decreases, the tendency to isolate oneself lessens, there are opportunities to reach out for help and support in times of stress, and there are opportunities to share mutual interests or experiences. Very importantly, others in recovery can offer the client strength, hope, and advice on ways to handle specific challenges of recovery such as how to manage cravings, deal with negative thinking about recovery, or make lifestyle changes necessary for long-term recovery.

In addition to specific people, organizations can be a major part of a client's recovery support system. Virtually any organization can be important to a given client. Possibilities include church, community, athletic, or recovery-oriented organizations, or those based on the specific needs and interests of the client. Chapter 15 in this guide focuses on self-help programs and recovery clubs, which play a crucial role in the recovery of many clients with substance use disorders.

There are, however, numerous barriers to asking for help and support. Clients whose social networks consist mainly of others who abuse or are dependent on alcohol or other drugs may be reluctant to cut their ties with these people, especially if they have long-term relationships. Some clients are so independent and self-reliant that they prefer to work things out on their own and don't like asking others for help or support, no matter how small the request may be. Others are shy, are socially anxious, lack self-confidence, or have poor social skills, making it difficult for them to know how to ask for help or support. In some instances, social anxiety and avoidant behavior are part of a more serious problem, such as a social phobia. These clients may not know whom to approach or even what to say. Yet others operate with the belief that they are not worthy of help from others or they will be rejected if they ask for it. Such beliefs create a barrier to building a recovery support system.

Objectives of the Session

1. To review the client's current social support system to identify the nature of current relationships

2. To identify the benefits of having a recovery support system

3. To identify specific individuals and organizations that the client can include in his or her support network

4. To help the client become aware of and overcome any specific barriers to asking for help and support

Major Points and Issues for Discussion

1. The therapist should review the client's current social network to get a perspective on his or her relationships. Do any significant relationships exist with others who actively abuse alcohol or other drugs? If so, how much of a threat do these relationships pose to the client's recovery? The therapist should find out whom the client trusts and who the client feels can provide him or her with help and support in his or her attempts to change.

2. The therapist should discuss the relationship between having a recovery support system and positive outcome in recovery. Clients who have support from family and friends generally do better in recovery than those who lack social support or who have negative social networks.

3. It is important to have a range of people—family members, friends, and others in recovery—in a recovery support system. The client should identify people who can offer support,

not those who will be negative, critical, or unsupportive of efforts to change.

The therapist should discuss the role that organizations (e.g., church, community) can play in the client's ongoing recovery. Find out organizations in which the client would like to be involved and discuss ways to go about this.

The client should complete the Recovery Network Worksheet (see Figure 14.1 in this guide and Chapter 13 in the Client Workbook). This worksheet will help the client identify specific people and organizations and the potential benefits of each in ongoing recovery. Some clients may be unable to identify relationships with people who do not have a substance use problem. If a client is unable to identify any specific person or organization that can support his or her recovery, the therapist and client need to explore the reasons for this. If necessary, the therapist can give specific suggestions on where the client may begin to establish some supportive relationships (e.g., at self-help meetings).

4. The therapist should point out that people in recovery sometimes have difficulty asking others for help and support. Some of the barriers to asking for help are (a) pride and excessive self-reliance, (b) shyness and intense social anxiety, (c) lack of social skills in communicating and interacting with others, (d) lack of self-confidence, and (e) negative beliefs about self (e.g., "I don't deserve for anyone to help me.") or others (e.g., "No one really cares about me" or "You can't depend on anyone else.").

If the client identifies these or other major barriers to reaching out to others, the therapist should discuss the reasons as well as strategies to overcome these barriers. Sometimes, changing beliefs will lead to a change in the client's behavior. In other instances, the client may need help in developing appropriate social skills such as initiating conversations, disclosing personal information about himself or herself, and making specific requests to others. Many clients know what they should do to elicit support but feel awkward, uncomfortable, or unworthy; others fail to ask for support because they simply do not know how.

A significant minority of clients with substance use disorders have high levels of social anxiety that lead them to avoid people, self-help programs, groups, or participation in community activities. Clients often don't spontaneously share this information;

Instructions: Identify people and organizations that you believe can be a vital part of your recovery network. Then, list the potential benefits of having these individuals and organizations as part of your recovery.

People/organizations	Potential benefits
Nurses recovery group	Chance to be with other nurses in recovery to talk about special problems we face; might feel more comfortable and able to talk about my drug problem; others have told me this group has been real helpful; can help me save my career in nursing.
NA meetings	Learn additional ways to stay drug free; place to talk about things bothering me; ways to meet drug-free people; can participate in NA-sponsored social events.
Linda (NA sponsor)	Can share personal things hard to bring up in groups; can share my small victories as well as struggles in recovery; she can help me with the 12-step program.
Parents	They've always been behind me and will do everything to support my recovery; regular visits will keep me close with them.
Sim and Terri	They've both been clean for a long time and can help me understand what to expect and how to stay clean; we can share support; and it will be safe to do social activities with them.

Figure 14.1. **Example of Completed Recovery Network Worksheet**

on the surface, they may appear resistant to actively developing a recovery support system. Self-administered questionnaires on anxiety, phobias, depression, or other problems can be used during the assessment process to identify clients who have significant levels of anxiety or avoidant behavior.

The therapist can encourage the client to participate in pleasant activities on a regular basis. Having fun and participating in normal social interactions makes the process of recovery more enjoyable and rewarding.

Chapter 15

Session Topic: Self-Help Programs and Recovery Clubs

Note: This session covers Chapter 14 in the Client Workbook.

Introduction

Self-help programs and recovery clubs are available to help clients in their ongoing recovery from substance use problems. The most common self-help programs are Alcoholics Anonymous (AA) and Narcotics Anonymous (NA). Some areas have other 12-step programs for specific types of drug abuse or dependence such as Cocaine Anonymous or Marijuana Anonymous.

There are also 12-step programs for clients who are trying to quit tobacco use, Smokers Anonymous and Nicotine Anonymous, but these are not available in many communities. A special 12-step program called Dual Recovery Anonymous (DRA) is available for clients who have both a substance use disorder and a psychiatric disorder. Unfortunately, DRA meetings are not as numerous as AA or NA meetings, and many areas have none at all.

Other self-help programs include Women for Sobriety (WFS), Men for Sobriety (MFS), Rational Recovery (RR), and Self-Management and Recovery Training (SMART). These programs are also less available than AA or NA, and some communities do not have any WFS, MFS, RR, or SMART groups at all.

Many areas have special clubs for people recovering from alcohol or drug problems. These clubs provide an atmosphere that is alcohol- and drug-free (except for cigarettes). Members can attend support group meetings and social events and interact informally with each other over a meal or cup of coffee.

A self-help program called Moderation Management is available for clients who have problems with alcohol but are not dependent and do not have serious psychiatric or medical problems. Moderation Management is also not recommended for clients who are taking medications that would interact adversely with alcohol. Moderation Management has a 9-step program of recovery that aims to help the client moderate alcohol use.

It helps to have as much firsthand information as possible about various self-help programs available in the client's community. Attending meetings that are open to the public, reading the literature, and talking with others who have attended self-help programs are excellent ways for the therapist to gain knowledge of self-help programs.

Although some clients participate throughout their lives in self-help programs, others use them for a specific period of time. Clients vary in their needs for involvement in self-help programs. Some are turned off by being told they have to maintain lifelong involvement.

As discussed in the previous chapter, some clients have high levels of social anxiety that make it difficult for them to attend meetings, talk during meetings, or initiate informal discussions with other members before, during, or after meetings. These clients may need help in challenging beliefs that prevent them from attending self-help meetings or help in learning social skills that make it easier for them to interact in group situations.

Objectives of the Session

1. To provide the client with information about self-help programs and recovery clubs

2. To help the client identify drawbacks and benefits of attending self-help programs and recovery clubs

3. To help the client identify specific self-help programs that can enhance his or her recovery

Major Points and Issues for Discussion

1. The therapist should discuss various self-help programs, recovery clubs, or clubhouses available in the client's area. The therapist can provide brochures, written descriptions, and recommendations

for books on specific programs, such as *Alcoholics Anonymous* (the "Big Book," 1976), *Narcotics Anonymous* (the "Basic Text," 1988), and *The Small Book* on Rational Recovery (Trimpey, 1992).

Self-help programs vary in their specific philosophy or approach to recovery, but most involve the following elements.

Fellowship. This involves people with similar problems helping each other deal with their alcohol or drug problems. People share experiences in and out of meetings, "sponsor" newcomers (commonly done in AA and NA), and are available to talk about recovery issues of mutual concern such as how to deal with cravings to use, how to recover from a lapse or relapse, and how to deal with the damage inflicted on others as a result of the substance use.

Recovery meetings. These involve discussions of a broad range of change issues or listening to others share their experiences with substance abuse and recovery.

Program steps or guidelines. These involve particular steps a client can take to deal with the alcohol or drug problem. Programs such as the 12 steps of AA and NA are seen by many as not only a way of overcoming a substance abuse problem, but as a way of life.

Self-help literature. Many booklets, books, and tapes are available to provide information, inspiration, or hope. Most are written by people recovering from an alcohol or drug problem.

Social events. Some self-help programs sponsor social activities such as holiday celebrations or sporting events. These activities provide an alcohol- and drug-free environment, which lessens the pressure to engage in substance use.

2. The client should complete the Self-Help Program Worksheet (see Figure 15.1 in this guide and Chapter 14 in the Client Workbook). On this worksheet, the client describes what it is like to ask for help, summarizes previous experiences in self-help programs, and identifies potential drawbacks and benefits of participating in self-help groups.

The therapist should discuss with the client his or her beliefs and attitudes about asking others for help and attending self-help programs, recovery clubs, or clubhouses. Many clients have unrealistic ideas about how these programs work or what is expected. For example, some believe that they have to stand in front of a crowd of strangers and publicly confess that they are an alcoholic or a drug addict.

Self-Help Program Worksheet

Instructions: Complete the following items to help you decide how self-help programs could help you stop using alcohol, tobacco, or other drugs and help reduce the chances of relapse.

1. Describe what it is like for you to ask others for help and support.

It's hard, I usually prefer working out my problems on my own.

2. Summarize your previous experiences in self-help programs (pro and con).

NA meetings were helpful because I learned ways to stay clean. The steps were hard, though, especially step 4. I did good until I blew off meetings and stopped completely.

3. List potential drawbacks of participating in self-help programs.

It's hard to find the time because of my work and family obligations. Some people are too intrusive. Others are phony.

4. List potential benefits of participating in self-help programs.

People are supportive, most don't judge you if you mess up, they know what works, the steps help you become a better person, and meetings are everywhere.

5. Which specific self-help program(s) do you think would benefit you in quitting or staying off alcohol, tobacco, or other drugs?

NA has worked the best for me.

Figure 15.1.   **Example of Completed Self-Help Program Worksheet**

The therapist should discuss with the client his or her previous involvement in self-help programs, recovery clubs, or clubhouses. What did the client find helpful and unhelpful? Even if a particular program wasn't helpful in the past, this doesn't mean that it cannot benefit the client at this time in his or her recovery.

The therapist should be respectful of the client's negative feelings about self-help programs, recovery clubs, or clubhouses. If a client can articulate why a particular program was not helpful before and why she doesn't wish to attend, other options should be considered.

The therapist should encourage skeptical clients to attend a certain number of self-help meetings, or even meetings for different groups before they make a final decision as to whether self-help programs can help. For example, we often ask clients to attend 6 to 12 meetings before reaching a final decision.

3. The therapist should let the client choose from among various self-help programs, recovery clubs, or clubhouses. How does the client perceive the pros and cons of each program? The therapist needs to be aware of his or her own biases. The therapist may not agree with a particular self-help group's philosophy or program, but it is up to the client to choose which group to attend.

    The therapist should provide lists of self-help programs or names of people to contact. Some clients are comfortable choosing programs from lists, but others feel more comfortable having a name of a specific individual to call. For many, having someone specific to contact eases the transition to a self-help group.

    The therapist should encourage the client to get a list of telephone numbers of other members of self-help groups and learn to reach out for help and support. In some instances, clients will need help learning social skills so that they can appropriately ask other people for support.

    The therapist should monitor the client's attendance of self-help programs and discuss the client's reactions, especially in the early stage of recovery. For example, a client may attend only one or two meetings and declare, "The program is not for me." Another client may focus on one particular person in a group who she feels is being dishonest or hypocritical, and judge the entire program based on this one individual.

If the client refuses to attend any self-help meetings, yet is unable to reach his goals with therapy, adjunctive medications, or both, the therapist should discuss with the client how another trial of self-help meetings may be beneficial.

Clients with significant levels of social anxiety and avoidant behavior may need specific help addressing their anxiety and avoidance before they will be ready to participate in self-help meetings. Therapists who cannot provide treatment for this type of problem should refer these clients to a speciality program, if available, or to a professional with expertise in treating social anxiety and social phobias.

Part 4

Relapse Prevention and Progress Measurement

Chapter 16

Session Topic: Reducing the Risk of Relapse

Note: This session covers Chapter 16 in the Client Workbook.

Introduction

Any client who attempts to modify alcohol, tobacco, or drug use behavior faces the possibility of lapse or relapse. A *lapse* refers to the initial episode of use following a period of abstinence. A lapse may involve limited use of a substance (e.g., a few drinks, cigarettes, or hits on a joint) or excessive use (e.g., actually getting intoxicated or high). A lapse may be quickly stopped by the client, or it may lead to a *relapse*, or continued use of a substance. How a client interprets and responds to a lapse plays a significant role in whether or not it leads to a relapse. For example, if a client feels extremely guilty and despondent over drinking after months of sobriety and tells herself, "I'm a failure" or "I'm not capable of stopping my alcohol use," she is likely to continue drinking. On the other hand, if a client tells himself, "I made a mistake and had better cut things off before they get worse," his lapse is less likely to lead to a relapse. In the latter example, the lapse turns into a *prolapse*, in which the client quickly uses positive coping strategies and learns something from the mistake that will aid ongoing recovery.

The risk of lapse or relapse is highest in the first 3 months of recovery, during which time about two out of three relapses occur. Often, though not always, a return to substance use is one decision among many that are made over a period of hours, days, or even longer. Many clients, for example, state that their relapse built up gradually and that actual substance use was preceded by relapse warning signs.

Low motivation and poor participation in therapy or self-help programs can raise the risk of relapse, even for clients who recently completed a rehabilitation program. Helping clients remain in therapy, identify early relapse warning signs, and identify high-risk situations are ways for the therapist to lower the client's risk of relapse.

Objectives of the Session

1. To introduce the client to the concepts of lapse and relapse in recovery from substance use disorders

2. To help the client learn about warning signs that frequently precede relapse and develop strategies to manage them

3. To help the client identify potential high-risk situations and strategies to cope with them

Major Points and Issues for Discussion

1. The therapist should discuss the difference between a lapse and a relapse and how the client's initial response to a lapse determines whether it leads to a relapse. What are the client's beliefs about relapse? Some clients believe they are invulnerable to relapse, believe they have learned their lesson so that relapse could never happen to them, or believe they don't need to make any changes in themselves or in their lifestyle to aid their long-term recovery.

2. The therapist should discuss the importance of identifying relapse warning signs. The earlier the client identifies potential or actual warning signs, the more able he or she will be to take action to prevent a relapse. The client should develop a plan *before* experiencing warning signs.

   The client needs to be educated about both obvious and subtle relapse warning signs, as well as about idiosyncratic warning signs. Idiosyncratic warning signs are those unique to each client in recovery. If the client has any previous experiences with relapse, these can be explored in detail to help him or her identify obvious and subtle warning signs. If the client is new to recovery, examples of common warning signs preceding substance use relapse can be reviewed.

A few examples of obvious relapse warning signs are (a) stopping or cutting down therapy sessions without making an agreement with the therapist that this is appropriate, (b) getting so busy that treatment-related activities are forgotten or given a low priority, (c) stopping or cutting down self-help meetings without discussing this decision with someone who knows about the client's recovery plan, (d) experiencing a significant increase in desires or thoughts of using and letting these build up, (e) stopping or decreasing other specific recovery behaviors (e.g., not completing a daily inventory, not participating in stress-reducing activities, not participating in pleasant activities, and (f) putting oneself in situations that are "set-ups" for relapse.

The client should complete the Relapse Warning Signs Worksheet (see Figure 16.1 in this guide and Chapter 16 in the Client Workbook). On this worksheet, the client lists potential warning signs and identifies strategies for managing them.

3. The therapist should emphasize the importance of anticipating and planning to cope with high-risk relapse situations as a way of better preparing for recovery. High-risk situations are those in which the client used alcohol, tobacco, or drugs in the past, as well as any situation in which the client's vulnerability to using substances is high.

The client needs to be educated about common categories of high-risk situations and to relate to these on a personal level so he or she can identify personal high-risk situations. The most common high-risk situations include (a) negative or upsetting emotional states; (b) social pressures to engage in substance use; (c) interpersonal conflict; (d) internal thoughts of using or a desire to "test" oneself; and (e) strong cravings for alcohol, tobacco, or other drugs.

The client should complete the High-Risk Situations Worksheet (see Figure 16.2 in this guide and Chapter 16 in the Client Workbook). Completing this worksheet will enable the client to begin identifying high-risk situations and positive coping strategies. The therapist can assess the client's coping skills to determine if there are specific deficits. For example, if a client identifies interpersonal disputes as a relapse risk and has a poor ability to negotiate differences with others, a deficit exists that raises his or her vulnerability to relapse and would be an appropriate target of therapy.

Instructions: In the left column, list the attitudes, thoughts, and behaviors that are warning signs of potential relapse. In the right column, write strategies for coping with each of these situations.

Relapse warning signs	Coping strategies
Begin to miss crack and the action of getting high.	Remind myself that the action of getting high caused girlfriend to leave. Getting high usually led to trouble in my life. Keep busy to limit free time on my hands. Join the Y to swim and play ball regularly.
Want to blow off NA meetings.	Talk it over with other NAs and sponsor. Examine real reasons for wanting to blow off meetings. Remind myself of benefits of meetings. Review track list of clean time to see how meetings are associated with staying clean.
Focus on new women instead of the NA program's steps.	Avoid going out after meetings alone with any new woman I meet. Don't give out my phone number or ask for phone numbers of women. Do an honesty check and ask myself what the real reasons are for this behavior.
Start to forget to do my daily review at the end of each day.	Figure out why I'm slacking off my program. Do my review before I get too tired and fall asleep, because I use this as an excuse. Keep a reminder note on the bathroom mirror to prompt me to take 10 minutes for my daily review.

Figure 16.1. **Example of Completed Relapse Warning Signs Worksheet**

Instructions: List three of your high-risk situations below. For each high-risk situation, list positive coping strategies.

High-risk situation 1	Coping strategies
I work too much and wear myself out.	Limiting long work days to no more than 2 each week. Take at least 1 full day off each week. Do something fun every single week. Take some time each day to relax and do whatever I want, including doing nothing. Tell myself I don't have to work all the time to prove I'm productive.

High-risk situation 2	Coping strategies
My boyfriend drinks a lot and likes us to go to bars and clubs, and we seem to argue a lot.	Reassess this relationship because he's not supporting my recovery; try to figure out why he'd want me to go, even though I'm trying to stay sober. In the meantime, don't go to bars or clubs, and suggest other social activities. Get to the bottom of why we're always at each other's throat, arguing and yelling. Stop my constant criticisms of him because this gets him going.

High-risk situation 3	Coping strategies
Feeling depressed about how my life is going.	Keep in mind that things are better since I got sober. Focus on one problem area at a time. Remember that I have a big say in how I feel, that I can take positive steps to change.

Figure 16.2. **Example of Completed High-Risk Situations Worksheet**

The therapist should use the information from the worksheet to help the client develop strategies for managing his or her high-risk situations. The focus should be on helping the client develop specific skills to deal with the problems identified. For example, if a client identified "angry feelings" as a major relapse threat and typically dealt with anger by internalizing it, she would need help in learning how to express anger appropriately in interpersonal situations. She may also need to change her beliefs about anger to facilitate learning new behavioral skills.

A daily inventory is one way for the client to continuously monitor high-risk situations. The therapist should encourage the client to take a few minutes at the end of each day to identify any current high-risk situations and develop plans to cope with them. For example, if an upcoming family visit during the holidays represented a high-risk situation for a client who was trying to abstain from alcohol, he could prepare to cope with the specific pressures he expected to face *before* making the trip. A "relapse roadmap" would help him chart his strategy ahead of time so that he would be better prepared to handle the situation. Waiting until he was actually with his family before planning relapse prevention might be too late.

Chapter 17

Session Topic: Relapse Management

Note: This session covers Chapter 17 in the Client Workbook.

Introduction

Even if clients are working toward total abstinence, they should be prepared to handle setbacks, because many clients who are attempting to quit alcohol, tobacco, or other drugs will use substances again. Knowing how to interrupt a lapse or relapse can help clients minimize damage associated with a return to substance use.

Lapses or relapses can be viewed as opportunities to learn from mistakes. Clients can use them to get back on track, change their recovery plan, or focus on learning new skills. As stated in the previous chapter, how a client responds to an initial lapse plays a significant role in whether the lapse leads to a relapse. Clients who lapse and then judge themselves harshly as failures or have strong feelings of demoralization are at risk to continue using substances. In addition to feeling like they let themselves down, clients may experience guilt and shame and feel that they let others down, including family, other friends in recovery, and even therapists.

Objectives of the Session

1. To help the client identify strategies to interrupt an actual lapse or relapse

2. To raise the client's awareness of his or her emotional and cognitive reactions to a lapse and how these reactions may lead to a relapse

3. To complete a "relapse debriefing" to help the client learn from his or her mistakes; this includes a review of the client's thoughts

and feelings, as well as the circumstances, events, or decisions
that led to the lapse or relapse

Major Points and Issues for Discussion

1. The therapist should discuss the importance of being able
   to interrupt a lapse or relapse in order to minimize the adverse
   effects on the client and his or her family. Usually, though
   not always, damage is minimized when the situation is controlled
   early. However, it may be very important for some clients
   to maintain abstinence. For example, physicians, other
   health care professionals, or athletes who are being monitored
   by a state regulatory agency could suffer tough consequences
   for one positive drug test, regardless of how small a quantity
   of the drug is detected.

   The therapist should help the client focus on strategies to catch
   setbacks as early as possible. Specific strategies can be rehearsed
   ahead of time so that the client feels more confident in his
   or her ability to use them. For example, a client may agree
   that a reasonable strategy to interrupt a lapse or relapse is to talk
   it over with a friend in a self-help program or with a therapist.
   However, the client may not be sure how to raise the issue
   or what to say, and may need guidance in how to disclose
   the experience.

2. If this is the client's first time in recovery, the therapist should
   ask him or her to imagine having a lapse, then describe his
   or her reactions to it. What could cause the lapse? What does
   the client feel after the initial episode of substance use? What
   does he or she think? What would happen next? What could
   the client do to stop the lapse from becoming a relapse?

3. If the client has experienced a lapse or relapse before,
   he or she should complete the Lapse and Relapse Worksheet
   (see Figure 17.1 in this guide and Chapter 17 in the Client
   Workbook). This worksheet will help the client identify the main
   reasons for the lapse, including thoughts, feelings, circumstances,
   or events that triggered the substance use. The client with
   a history of multiple relapses should complete this worksheet
   for several recent relapses. Are there any patterns to the client's
   lapses or relapses in terms of warning signs, where and when they
   occur, how long they last, and their impact on the client's life?

The therapist should review the concept of relapse as a process and state that actual substance use is the last link in a chain. Earlier links represent specific relapse warning signs or decisions that led the client away from recovery and toward relapse. The client who has had a relapse should complete the Relapse Chain Worksheet (see Figure 17.2 in this guide and Chapter 17 in the Client Workbook). In addition to helping identify warning signs that preceded a past relapse, this worksheet also helps the client figure out how much time may have elapsed between early warning signs and actual substance use. In some instances, the process is quick; in other cases, early warning signs may precede actual substance use by weeks or months.

The therapist should discuss the actual and potential effects of a lapse or relapse. If the client has had lapses or relapses, he or she can describe the effects of the lapse or relapse on his or her life and significant relationships.

Because it isn't unusual for family members or significant others to react negatively to a client's substance use, have the client discuss his or her experiences with others' reactions. If the client has not had a lapse or relapse, he or she can think of potential reactions of family or significant others. Unfortunately, in some instances, clients may pay a steep price for a lapse or relapse. For example, a client's partner may end the relationship if the client uses drugs following a period of recovery.

Instructions: Answer the following questions to help you figure out what led to your first drink, cigarette, or other drug use after having quit.

1. Describe the main reason you took the first drink, cigarette, or other drug.

I smoked again because I wanted one real bad. It was a hard day at work.

2. Describe your inner thoughts and feelings that triggered your need or desire for the first drink, cigarette, or other drug.

I felt anxious and tense, I thought I deserved something to relax me and calm me down after the day I had at work.

3. Describe any external circumstances that triggered your need or desire for the first drink, cigarette, or other drug.

My husband started an argument with me over the budget. He said it was my fault we had so many bills. This made me mad.

4. Describe the first decision you made that started the lapse or relapse process.

I decided to hide the budget from my husband for a few days even though I knew this would lead to an argument and problems down the road.

Figure 17.1.   Examples of Completed Lapse and Relapse Worksheets

Instructions: Answer the following questions to help you figure out what led to your first drink, cigarette, or other drug use after having quit.

1. Describe the main reason you took the first drink, cigarette, or other drug.

I went out on a date with this guy I really liked. He suggested a certain wine with our dinner so I didn't bother to tell him I was trying to stay off booze.

2. Describe your inner thoughts and feelings that triggered your need or desire for the first drink, cigarette, or other drug.

I felt excited to be with him and didn't want to disappoint him because he seemed to know so much about wine. I thought it seemed silly that I couldn't have a glass or two of wine with dinner.

3. Describe any external circumstances that triggered your need or desire for the first drink, cigarette, or other drug.

I wanted to get to know this man better and thought a few glasses of wine would make it easier to open up to him.

4. Describe the first decision you made that started the lapse or relapse process.

I decided to go out on a date with a man that I was pretty sure was a drinker.

Figure 17.1. **Examples of Completed Lapse and Relapse Worksheets** (*continued*)

Instructions: Answer the following questions to help you figure out what led to your first drink, cigarette, or other drug use after having quit.

1. Describe the main reason you took the first drink, cigarette, or other drug.

I felt pressure to fit in with my friends who were drinking and using cocaine. I wanted to be one of the guys and not stick out because I wasn't getting high.

2. Describe your inner thoughts and feelings that triggered your need or desire for the first drink, cigarette, or other drug.

I felt awkward, plus it was boring to watch the guys have a good time getting high. I thought what the hell, I'll just have a few beers. Don't use cocaine and I'll be cool.

3. Describe any external circumstances that triggered your need or desire for the first drink, cigarette, or other drug.

Once I drank a few beers, it was only a matter of time until I snorted some coke. The high from the beer wasn't good enough and I had to have cocaine. Soon, I was using regularly.

4. Describe the first decision you made that started the lapse or relapse process.

I decided that I could hang out with the guys and not use cocaine; that as long as I watched myself, I would be OK.

Figure 17.1. **Examples of Completed Lapse and Relapse Worksheets** *(continued)*

Relapse Chain Worksheet

Instructions: The last link in the relapse chain represents your use of alcohol, tobacco, or other drugs. Each preceding link represents a specific relapse warning sign. Identify as many warning signs as you can. Then state how much time elapsed between the earliest warning sign and the first time you used a substance again. Also, state how you felt about using substances again, and how your family (or other significant people in your life) felt.

Found a couple of joints in my drawer when looking for a sweater.

Thought a few hits would be nice, but didn't use any, put joint back in drawer.

Didn't make any weekend plans.

At work, thought about what a drag the weekend had been.

Called Arlene who invited me to a party on Saturday.

Told myself I was ready for a party, that if I couldn't go and not get high, I'd never beat this thing.

Went to her party.

Invited Arlene over to my house the next week for lunch.

She asked me if I'd mind if she smoked a joint, I said go ahead.

After she lit up, I took a few hits and later went out for a few drinks.

Time elapsed from early warning signs to actual use: _3 weeks_

How I felt about using again: _Excited at first, then guilty and shameful._

How my family or significant others felt: _Upset, disappointed, and angry._

Figure 17.2.   **Example of Completed Relapse Chain Worksheet**

Chapter 18

Session Topic: Strategies for Balanced Living

Note: This session covers Chapter 18 in the Client Workbook.

Introduction

Achieving balance in the various dimensions of life can protect the client from relapse. The more balanced and satisfying a client's life is, the less the client needs to use substances to feel good, escape, gain excitement, or cope with problems. Balance refers to the client's ability to meet his or her responsibilities or obligations and to take care of his or her unique personal needs and wants. A balanced lifestyle involves the ability to reasonably balance various aspects of life: physical, emotional, intellectual, creative, family, interpersonal, spiritual, work or school, and financial. Balanced living also contributes to personal growth and happiness.

Because life is full of demands and responsibilities, it isn't unusual for some areas of life to become unbalanced from time to time. The important issue for the client is living with temporary periods of imbalance when they are unavoidable or necessary and working toward better balance when possible.

Objectives of the Session

1. To help the client evaluate the major dimensions of life to determine which areas are out of balance and how to work toward better balance

2. To teach the client how to use a daily inventory to catch problems that could lead to imbalance in life

3. To teach the client how to build structure and pleasant activities into daily life

Major Points and Issues for Discussion

1. The therapist should discuss the concept of balance in life from two perspectives: (a) need for balance between obligations and wants, and (b) need for balance and satisfaction among the major dimensions of life (work, family, relationships, etc.).

   The client should complete the Teeter-Totter Balance Test (see Figure 18.1 in this guide and Chapter 18 in the Client Workbook). This exercise will provide a global overview of the client's obligations versus his or her needs.

   Balanced living can help raise the client's level of satisfaction with his or her life and reduce the risk of relapse. If imbalance is too great, and the client is overwhelmed by too many obligations or pressures, the temptation to escape or experience pleasure through substance use may increase. To address this issue, the client should look at all areas of life to determine which ones are out of balance and need attention. Once identified, areas of imbalance can be targeted for change.

   The client should complete the Lifestyle Balance Worksheet (see Figure 18.2 in this guide and Chapter 18 in the Client Workbook). This worksheet poses a number of questions in nine major areas of life functioning. The client's answers to these questions will help determine which of the following areas are out of balance and need to be worked on: physical, mental

Teeter-Totter Balance Test

Wants List	Shoulds List
Take fun breaks at work	Go to work
Buy myself a treat	Pay bills
Go to a movie after chores	Do chores
Plan a vacation	Take care of relatives

Figure 18.1.   **Example of Completed Teeter-Totter Balance Test**

or emotional, intellectual, creative or artistic, family, personal relationships, spiritual, work or school, and financial.

Some periods of imbalance are inevitable due to demands of daily living or particular circumstances. For example, a client who is both working full-time and attending school will need to devote sufficient time to studying in order to meet his or her goals. This may mean that other areas, such as social relationships or creative and artistic endeavors, are put on hold or given less time and attention. A client who is a new parent is likely to have much less time to pursue personal interests than he or she would like due to the demands of child-rearing. The challenge is for the client not to totally ignore areas of life that are important to his or her well-being.

The therapist should help the client prioritize out-of-balance areas that need to be changed. The therapist and client should work collaboratively to develop reasonable strategies for addressing issues or problems.

2. Using a daily inventory or review is one way the client can catch problems before they cause imbalance in life (see Chapter 18 in the Client Workbook). A daily inventory can help the client monitor progress on a daily basis.

3. If the client needs to build more structure into his or her life, he or she should complete the Weekly Schedule Worksheet (see Chapter 18 in the Client Workbook). This is another way to identify and address the issue of lifestyle balance. For example, a client may be spending a disproportionate amount of time at work-related activities at the expense of important relationships or leisure activities. Although structure is often helpful, it is also important to have some unstructured time.

One way for the client to work toward balance between obligations and needs is to complete the Pleasant Activities Worksheet (see Figure 18.3 in this guide and Chapter 18 in the Client Workbook). On this worksheet, the client lists current activities that he or she enjoys, as well as new, pleasant activities to try. This exercise can help the client identify and plan new activities that are fun or enjoyable or add to better balance in life. As simple as this sounds, however, it isn't unusual for clients to struggle in pursuing a new activity. Clients create many excuses for why a new activity cannot be pursued. The therapist can help the client anticipate some of these roadblocks and better prepare him or her for change.

Instructions: Answer the following questions to help you determine how balanced your life is currently. Then review your answers. Identify two out-of-balance areas that you want to change. Write a plan for change in each area.

1. Physical:

Are you in good health?	✔ Yes	____ No
Do you exercise regularly?	____ Yes	✔ No
Do you follow a reasonable diet?	✔ Yes	____ No
Do you take good care of your appearance?	✔ Yes	____ No
Do you get sufficient rest and sleep?	✔ Yes	____ No
Do you get regular medical and dental checkups?	✔ Yes	____ No
Do you have strategies to handle cravings to use substances?	✔ Yes	____ No

2. Mental/emotional:

Are you experiencing excessive stress?	____ Yes	✔ No
Do you worry too much?	____ Yes	✔ No
Do you have strategies to reduce mental stress?	✔ Yes	____ No
Are you able to express your feelings to others?	____ Yes	✔ No
Do you suffer from serious depression or anxiety?	____ Yes	✔ No

3. Intellectual:

Are you able to satisfy your intellectual needs?	✔ Yes	____ No
Do you have enough interests to satisfy your intellectual curiosity?	✔ Yes	____ No

4. Creative/artistic:

Do you regularly participate in creative or artistic endeavors?	____ Yes	✔ No
Do you have talents or abilities that you think are not being used as much as you would like?	✔ Yes	____ No

5. Family:

Are you generally satisfied with your family relationships?	✔ Yes	____ No
Do you spend enough time with your family (especially your children, if you have any)?	____ Yes	✔ No
Can you rely on your family for help and support?	✔ Yes	____ No

6. Personal relationships:

Are you generally satisfied with the quantity and quality of your personal relationships?	✔ Yes	____ No
Do you have friends you can depend on for help and support?	✔ Yes	____ No
Are you able to express your ideas, needs, and feelings to others?	✔ Yes	____ No
Are there any specific relationships in which you have serious problems?	____ Yes	✔ No

Figure 18.2. Example of Completed Lifestyle Balance Worksheet

7. Spiritual:

Is there enough love in your life?	✔ Yes	___ No
Do you pay enough attention to your "inner" spiritual life?	✔ Yes	___ No
Do you feel a sense of inner peace?	___ Yes	✔ No

8. Work or school:

Are you usually satisfied with your work or school situation?	___ Yes	✔ No
Do you spend too much time or effort working?	✔ Yes	___ No
Do you spend too little time or effort working?	___ Yes	✔ No

9. Financial:

Do you have sufficient income to meet your expenses?	✔ Yes	___ No
Are you having any serious financial problems (e.g., too much debt, no savings, etc.)?	___ Yes	✔ No
Do you handle your money responsibilities with an eye to the future?	✔ Yes	___ No
Does money play too big a role in your life?	___ Yes	✔ No

Out-of-balance area:
I don't spend enough time with my family.

My change plan:
Have dinner with my family at least 3 evenings during the week.
Plan family activities at least once each weekend.
Take my wife out alone at least once a month.
Spend at least 1 hour each week alone with each of my kids.
Plan a weekend trip with my family.

Out-of-balance area:
I spend too much time working.

My change plan:
Work late only 2 days per week.
Carefully keep track of how much time I work.
Delegate more work to employees I supervise.
Limit work I do at home on weekends to one block of time on Saturday.
Get back to playing tennis every week and avoid being too busy at work as an excuse for why I can't play.

Figure 18.2. **Example of Completed Lifestyle Balance Worksheet** (*continued*)

Instructions: List current activities that you consider to be a pleasant part of your life. Then, think of several new activities to try. These should be activities in which there is no or minimal pressure to use alcohol or other drugs.

Current pleasant activities

Jogging
Going to new movies
Watching old movies
Visiting friends
Visiting my sister and her family
Reading novels
Playing with my children
Coffee in the morning with my husband
Reading the paper after dinner
Watching the news before bedtime
Taking hot baths

New pleasant activities

Learn how to ski
Go to a jazz concert with my husband
Go swimming with my children
Learn how to use the Internet on the computer
Read biographies of people I admire

Figure 18.3.   **Example of Completed Pleasant Activities Worksheet**

Chapter 19

Session Topic: Measuring Progress

Note: This session covers Chapter 19 in the Client Workbook.

Introduction

Progress in recovery is measured according to the client's goals.
It is helpful for the client to periodically review his or her progress
and check it against his or her goals; this helps the client to see
if he or she is making progress and to identify new goals and recovery
strategies. Clients sometimes minimize their progress, especially when
they have temporary setbacks. Viewing progress realistically helps
improve the client's motivation to continue working toward recovery
and reinforces the client for positive changes, no matter how small.

There are many ways to measure progress. Although the ideal goal is total
abstinence from alcohol or other drugs, any movement toward this goal
can be viewed as progress. For example, a client who comes to treatment
with very little interest in changing substance use behavior, then begins
to rethink this position and examine his substance use, is making
progress. Another client who was a daily user is abstinent for several
weeks or months. Even though she has a relapse, this client is still moving
in the right direction and making progress.

In some instances, progress is large and obvious. In other instances,
it has to be measured in small changes. Progress can be measured in terms
of cessation or reduction of substance use as well as in other areas.

Objectives of the Session

1. To help the client evaluate progress against goals identified
    in his or her change plan

2. To help the client be realistic about ways in which to measure progress

3. To help the client modify "all or none" beliefs about progress in order to appreciate small changes

Major Points and Issues for Discussion

1. The therapist and client should review the client's progress to date. Progress should be discussed in relation to the treatment goals outlined in the original change plan. The discussion should be balanced between positive steps made to date and changes the client still wants to make. The client should review progress often during the initial weeks or months of recovery (e.g., weekly at first).

   If the client is unable to make any progress with the current plan, other treatment options should be discussed. For example, if a client couldn't make any headway on his alcohol problem with weekly or biweekly therapy sessions, the frequency of sessions could be increased, or a more intensive level of treatment, such as an intensive outpatient program, could be considered. Adding treatments to the existing plan (e.g., taking ReVia, participating in a therapy group in addition to individual sessions) could also be considered.

   If the client's treatment will be terminated, the therapist should review the client's plan for continued, post-treatment change.

2. Although each client needs to measure progress against his or her personal goals, any of the following milestones indicates that progress is being made: (a) The client is moving from one stage of the change process to another (e.g., from contemplation to preparation, from preparation to action); (b) the client is able to maintain abstinence from alcohol or other drugs; (c) the client reduces the amount and frequency of substance use; (d) the client experiences a decrease in the harmful effects of substance use; (e) the client's health or life has improved in one or more ways (e.g., physical health, spirituality, relationships); (f) the client experiences a decrease in obsessions and cravings to use substances; (g) the client feels more hopeful or confident about his or her ability to make positive changes and handle problems; (h) the client is more aware of high-risk situations, is willing to discuss them,

and has a plan to cope with them; (i) the client is willing to discuss setbacks in detail in order to learn from them; (j) the client cuts off a lapse or relapse more quickly than in the past; (k) the client is able to use a variety of strategies or skills to cope with problems and challenges in recovery; or (l) the client is willing to alter his or her change plan if the current approach is not working effectively.

The client should get feedback from others about his or her progress. For example, sponsors or friends in recovery who know the client well or family members who are aware of the client's recovery process can point out ways in which he or she is making progress.

3. The therapist should help the client avoid the common trap of judging progress in absolute, "all or none" terms. Otherwise, unless the client makes substantial changes, he or she may feel demoralized, give up, or judge himself or herself to be incapable of change. The therapist should discuss ways in which the client can reward himself or herself for positive changes made, no matter how small.

The client should reward himself or herself for efforts to change as well as actual changes. Many people work hard, only to stumble on the way to change. However, putting forth a good effort can be a positive experience as long as the effort is not overlooked and taken for granted. Trying to change and failing is better than not trying to change at all.

Case Studies

Mike (Alcohol)

Mike is a 38-year-old, self-employed, married father of two children who has been in three rehabilitation programs and two outpatient programs for alcoholism during the past 7 years. He has been alcohol-free for over 5 months, the longest he's ever been sober. Mike attends AA meetings regularly and talks openly about his occasional desires to drink alcohol. He has not missed any outpatient therapy sessions in the last 5 months, a big improvement compared to the past, when he seldom kept his appointments and dropped out of treatment early only to relapse again. Whereas his marriage had been on the brink of falling apart, he and his wife are getting along well now. Mike has taken an active role with his children, too. Clearly, he's made many strides in his recovery to date.

Lana (Marijuana)

Lana is a 26-year-old secretary with a 5-year history of marijuana abuse. At her worst, she was smoking several joints a day. Lana is frustrated because she feels her life hasn't gotten any better since she quit smoking marijuana 8 months ago. However, when she and her therapist closely examined her life, Lana discovered that she is better off in several ways now that she's drug-free: she has not missed work at all since stopping drugs, whereas before, she routinely used all of her sick leave early in the year; she has saved several hundred dollars each month, compared to previously saving nothing; she's planning to go back to night school because she wants to get a better paying job and establish a different career; and her overall mood is slightly better than when she smoked marijuana regularly.

Lindsey (Tobacco)

Lindsey is a 51-year-old millwright with a lifelong pattern of smoking up to three packs of cigarettes a day. He first quit smoking over a year ago at the advice of his family doctor. Lindsey has had two lapses and one relapse since this time, lasting from 1 day to 4 weeks. During the 4-week relapse, he smoked daily, but seldom more than a pack a day—a big improvement over the past. He realized from these experiences that he cannot safely smoke a limited number of cigarettes. Lindsey also realized that he has more stamina when he doesn't smoke and that his wife is more affectionate when he doesn't reek of cigarettes.

Appendix

Self-Help Organizations and Publishers

Al-Anon Family Group
Headquarters, Inc.
1600 Corporate Landing Parkway
Virginia Beach, VA 23454-5617
(800) 344-2666

Alcoholics Anonymous World
Services, Inc.
P.O. Box 459
New York, NY 10163
(212) 870-3400

Gerald T. Rogers Productions
1000 Skokie Boulevard, Suite 575
Wilmette, IL 60091-1154
(800) 227-9100

Hazelden Foundation
C.O.3, P.O. Box 11
Center City, MN 55012-0011
(800) 257-7810

Moderation Management
Network, Inc.
P.O. Box 27558
Golden Valley, MN 55427
(612) 512-1484

Narcotics Anonymous World Service
Office
P.O. Box 9999
Van Nuys, CA 91409
(818) 773-9999

The National Association for Children
of Alcoholics
11426 Rockville Pike, Suite 100
Rockville, MD 20852
(888) 554-COAS; (888) 554-2627

National Clearinghouse for Alcohol
and Drug Information (NCADI)
P.O. Box 2345
Rockville, MD 20847-2345
(800) SAY-NOTO; (800) 729-6686

The Psychological Corporation
555 Academic Court
San Antonio, TX 78204-2498
(800) 228-0752

Self-Management and Recovery
Training (SMART)
24000 Mercantile Road, Suite 11
Beachwood, OH 44122
(216) 292-0220

Suggested Additional Readings

Alling, F. A. (1992). Detoxification and treatment of acute sequelae. In J. H. Lowinson, P. Ruiz, & R. B. Millman (Eds.), *Substance abuse: A comprehensive textbook* (2nd ed., pp. 402–415). Baltimore: Williams & Wilkins.

Alterman, A. I., O'Brien, C. P., & McLellan, A. T. (1991). Differential therapeutics for substance abuse. In R. J. Frances & S. I. Miller (Eds.), *Clinical textbook of addictive disorders* (pp. 369–390). New York: The Guilford Press.

Anthenelli, R. M., & Schuckit, M. A. (1992). Genetics. In J. H. Lowinson, P. Ruiz, & R. B. Millman (Eds.), *Substance abuse: A comprehensive textbook* (2nd ed., pp. 39–50). Baltimore: Williams & Wilkins.

Beck, A. T. (1976). *Cognitive therapy and the emotional disorders.* New York: New American Library.

Beck, A. T., Wright, F. D., Newman, C. F., & Liese, B. S. (1993). *Cognitive therapy of substance abuse.* New York: The Guilford Press.

Brown, S. (Ed.). (1995). *Treating alcoholism.* San Francisco: Jossey-Bass.

Brownell, K. (1998). *The L.E.A.R.N. Program for weight control.* Dallas, TX: American Health.

Burns, D. D. (1989). *The feeling good handbook.* New York: Penguin.

Childress, A. R., Ehrman, R., Rohsenow, D. J., Robbins, S. J., & O'Brien, C. P. (1992). Classically conditioned factors in drug dependence. In J. H. Lowinson, P. Ruiz, & R. B. Millman (Eds.), *Substance abuse: A comprehensive textbook* (2nd ed., pp. 56–69). Baltimore: Williams & Wilkins.

Daley, D. C. (1986). *Relapse prevention workbook.* Holmes Beach, FL : Learning Publications.

Daley, D. C. (1987). *Family recovery workbook.* Bradenton, FL: Human Services Institute.

Daley, D. C. (Ed.). (1988). *Relapse: Conceptual, research and clinical perspectives.* New York: The Haworth Press.

Daley, D. C. (1988). *Relapse prevention: Treatment alternatives and counseling aids.* Bradenton, FL: Human Services Institute.

Daley, D. C. (1988). *Surviving addiction: A guide for alcoholics, drug addicts, and their families.* New York: Gardner Press.

Daley, D. C. (1992). *Coping with anger workbook.* Skokie, IL: Gerald T. Rogers.

Daley, D. C. (1994). *Living sober: An interactive video recovery program—client workbook.* Wilmette, IL: Gerald T. Rogers.

Daley, D. C. (1996). *Coping with feelings workbook.* Holmes Beach, FL: Learning Publications.

Daley, D. C. (1996). *Living sober II: An interactive video recovery program—counseling manual.* Wilmette, IL: Gerald T. Rogers.

Daley, D. C., Moss, H., & Campbell, F. (1993). *Dual disorders: Counseling clients with chemical dependency and mental illness* (2nd ed.). Center City, MN: Hazelden.

Daley, D. C., & Thase, M. E. (1994). *Dual disorders recovery counseling: A biopsychosocial treatment model for addiction and psychiatric illness.* Independence, MO: Herald House/Independence Press.

DuPont Pharma. (1995). *ReVia naltrexone HCI.* [Brochure]. U.S.A.:Author.

Earley, P. H. (1991). *The cocaine recovery book.* Newbury Park, CA: Sage.

Ellis, A., McInerney, J. F., DiGiuseppe, R., & Yeager, R. J. (1988). *Rational-emotive therapy with alcoholics and substance abusers.* Elmsford, NY: Pergamon Press.

Flores, P. J. (1988). *Group psychotherapy with addicted populations.* New York: The Haworth Press.

Galanter, M. (1992). Office management of the substance abuser: The use of learning theory and social networks. In J. H. Lowinson, P. Ruiz, & R. B. Millman (Eds.), *Substance abuse: A comprehensive textbook* (2nd ed., pp. 543–549). Baltimore: Williams & Wilkins.

Gerstley, L., McLellan, A. T., Alterman, A. I., Woody, G. E., Luborsky, L., & Prout, M. (1989). Ability to form an alliance with the therapist: A possible marker of prognosis for patients with antisocial personality disorder. *The American Journal of Psychiatry, 146*(4), 508–512.

Gorski, T. T., & Miller, M. (1986). *Staying sober: A guide for relapse prevention.* Independence, MO: Independence Press.

Greenberger, D., & Padesky, C. A. (1995). *Mind over mood: A cognitive therapy treatment manual for clients.* New York: The Guilford Press.

Greenstein, R. A., Fudala, P. J., & O'Brien, C. P. (1992). Alternative pharmacotherapies for opiate addiction. In J. H. Lowinson, P. Ruiz, & R. B. Millman (Eds.), *Substance abuse: A comprehensive textbook* (2nd ed., pp. 562–573). Baltimore: Williams & Wilkins.

Hamilton, T., & Samples, P. (1994). *The twelve steps and dual disorders.* Center City, MN: Hazelden.

Hester, R. K., & Miller, W. R. (Eds.). (1995). *Handbook of alcoholism treatment approaches: Effective alternatives* (2nd ed.). Boston: Allyn & Bacon.

Jarvik, M. E., & Schneider, N. G. (1992). Nicotine. In J. H. Lowinson, P. Ruiz, & R. B. Millman (Eds.), *Substance abuse: A comprehensive textbook* (2nd ed., pp. 334–356). Baltimore: Williams & Wilkins.

Johnson, B. D., & Muffler, J. (1992). Sociocultural aspects of drug use and abuse in the 1990s. In J. H. Lowinson, P. Ruiz, & R. B. Millman (Eds.), *Substance abuse: A comprehensive textbook* (2nd ed., pp. 118–137). Baltimore: Williams & Wilkins.

Jones, C. L., & Battjes, R. J. (1985). *Etiology of drug abuse: Implications for prevention* (National Institute on Drug Abuse Research Monograph Series, No. 56). (DHHS Publication No. ADM 85–1335). Washington, DC: U.S. Government Printing Office.

Kadden, R., Carroll, K., Donovan, D., Cooney, N., Monti, P., Abrams, D., Litt, M., & Hester, R. (Eds.). (1995). *Cognitive-behavioral coping skills therapy manual: A clinical research guide for therapists treating individuals with alcohol abuse and dependence* (National Institute on Alcohol Abuse and Alcoholism Project MATCH Monograph Series, Vol. 3). (NIH Publication No. 94-3724). Rockville, MD: National Institute on Alcohol Abuse and Alcoholism.

Kaufman, E. (1992). Family therapy: A treatment approach with substance abusers. In J. H. Lowinson, P. Ruiz, & R. B. Millman (Eds.), *Substance abuse: A comprehensive textbook* (2nd ed., pp. 520–532). Baltimore: Williams & Wilkins.

Kaufman, E., & Kaufmann, P.(Eds.). (1979). *Family therapy of drug and alcohol abuse.* New York: Gardner Press.

Kishline, A. (1994). *Moderate drinking: The new option for problem drinkers.* Tucson, AZ: See Sharp Press.

Kosten, T. R. (1992). Pharmacotherapies. In T. R. Kosten & H. D. Kleber (Eds.), *Clinician's guide to cocaine addiction: Theory, research, and treatment* (pp. 273–289). New York: The Guilford Press.

Lowinson, J. H., Marion, I. J., Joseph H., & Dole, V. P. (1992). Methadone maintenance. In J. H. Lowinson, P. Ruiz, & R. B. Millman (Eds.), *Substance abuse: A comprehensive textbook* (2nd ed., pp. 550–561). Baltimore: Williams & Wilkins.

Luborsky, L. (1984). *Principles of psychoanalytic psychotherapy: A manual for supportive-expressive treatment.* New York: Basic Books.

Marlatt, G. A., & Gordon, J. R. (Eds.). (1985). *Relapse prevention: Maintenance strategies in the treatment of addictive behaviors.* New York: The Guilford Press.

Marlatt, G. A., & Tapert, S. F. (1993). Harm reduction: Reducing the risks of addictive behaviors. In J. S. Baer, G. A. Marlatt, & R. J. McMahon (Eds.), *Addictive behaviors across the life span: Prevention, treatment, and policy issues* (pp. 243–273). Newbury Park, CA: Sage.

Miller, W. R., Zweben, A., DiClemente, C. C., & Rychtarik, R. G. (1994). Motivational enhancement therapy manual. *A clinical research guide for therapists treating individuals with alcohol abuse and dependence* (National Institute on Alcohol Abuse and Alcoholism Project MATCH Monograph Series,Vol. 2). (NIH Publication No. 94-3723). Rockville, MD: National Institute on Alcohol Abuse and Alcoholism.

Monti, P. M., Abrams, D. B., Kadden, R. M., & Cooney, N. L. (1989). *Treating alcohol dependence: A coping skills training guide.* New York: The Guilford Press.

National Institute on Drug Abuse. (1993). *Cue extinction: In-service training curriculum* (NIH Publication No. 93-3692). Rockville, MD: Author.

National Institute on Drug Abuse. (1993). *Recovery training and self-help: Relapse prevention and aftercare for drug addicts* (NIH Publication No. 93-3521). Rockville, MD: Author.

Nowinski, J., Baker, S., & Carroll, K. (1992). *Twelve step facilitation therapy manual: A clinical research guide for therapists treating individuals with alcohol abuse and dependence* (National Institute on Alcohol Abuse and Alcoholism Project MATCH Monograph Series, Vol. 1). (DHHS Publication No. ADM 92-1893). Rockville, MD: National Institute on Alcohol Abuse and Alcoholism.

O'Farrell, T. J., Allen, J. P., & Litten, R. Z. (1995). Disulfiram (Antabuse) contracts in treatment of alcoholism. In L. S. Onken, J. D. Blaine, & J. J. Boren (Eds.), *Integrating behavioral therapies with medication in the treatment of drug dependence* (National Institute on Drug Abuse Research Monograph Series No. 150, pp. 65–91). (NIH Publication No. 95-3899). Washington, DC: U.S. Government Printing Office.

Onken, L. S., & Blaine, J. D. (1990). *Psychotherapy and counseling in the treatment of drug abuse* (NIDA Research Monograph No. 104). Washington, DC: U.S. Government Printing Office.

Onken, L. S., Blaine, J. D. & Boren, J. J. (Eds.). (1995). *Integrating behavioral therapies with medications in the treatment of drug dependence* (National Institute on Drug Abuse Research Monograph Series No. 150). (NIH Publication No. 95-3899). Washington, DC : U.S. Government Printing Office.

Ray, B. A. (Ed.). (1988). *Learning factors in substance abuse* (National Institute on Drug Abuse Research Monograph Series No. 84). (DHHS Publication No. ADM 88-1576). Washington, DC: U.S. Government Printing Office.

Rounsaville, B. J., & Carroll, K. M. (1992). Individual psychotherapy for drug abusers. In J. H. Lowinson, P. Ruiz, & R. B. Millman (Eds.), *Substance abuse: A comprehensive textbook* (2nd ed., pp. 496–507). Baltimore: Williams & Wilkins.

Rounsaville, B. J., & Carroll, K. (1993). Interpersonal psychotherapy for patients who abuse drugs. In G. Klerman & M. Weissman (Eds.), *New applications of interpersonal psychotherapy* (pp. 319–352). Washington, DC: American Psychiatric Press.

Rustin, T. A. (1994). *Quit and stay quit: A personal program to stop smoking.* Center City, MN: Hazelden.

S.M.A.R.T.: Self-management and recovery training workbook. (1995). San Diego, CA.

Stanton, M. D., & Todd, T. C. (1982). *The family therapy of drug abuse and addiction.* New York: The Guilford Press.

The Neurobehavioral Treatment Model (Vols. I & II). (1989). Beverly Hills, CA: The Matrix Center.

U.S. Department of Health and Human Services. (1993). Diagnosis and treatment of alcoholism. In *Eighth special report to the U.S. Congress on alcohol and health from the Secretary of Health and Human Services* (pp. 319–349). Washington, DC: U.S. Government Printing Office.

Verebey, K., & Turner, C. E. (1991). Laboratory testing. In R. J. Frances & S. I. Miller (Eds.), *Clinical textbook of addictive disorders* (pp. 221–236). New York: The Guilford Press.

Washton, A. M. (Ed.). (1995). *Psychotherapy and substance abuse: A practitioner's handbook.* New York: The Guilford Press.

Zackon, F., McAuliffe, W. E., & Ch'ien, J. M. N. (1993). *Recovery training and self-help: Relapse prevention and aftercare for drug addicts.* (NIH Publication No. 93-3521). Rockville, MD: National Institute on Drug Abuse.

References

Alcoholics anonymous: The story of how many thousands of men and women have recovered from alcoholism (3rd ed.). (1976). New York: AA World Services, Inc.

American Psychiatric Association. (1994). Substance-related disorders. In *Diagnostic and statistical manual of mental disorders* (4th ed., pp. 175–272). Washington, DC: Author.

American Psychiatric Association. (1995). Practice guidelines for the treatment of patients with substance use disorders: Alcohol, cocaine, opioids. *American Journal of Psychiatry, 152*(11) (Suppl.).

Carroll, J. F. (1984). The Substance Abuse Problem Checklist: A new clinical aid for drug and/or alcohol treatment dependency. *Journal of Substance Abuse Treatment, 1*(1), 31–36.

Daley, D. C., & Marlatt, G. A. (1992). Relapse prevention: Cognitive and behavioral interventions. In J. H. Lowinson, P. Ruiz, & R. B. Millman (Eds.), *Substance abuse: A comprehensive textbook* (2nd ed., pp. 533–542). Baltimore: Williams & Wilkins.

Hoffman, N. G., Halikas, J. A., Mee-Lee, D., & Weedman, R. D. (1991). *ASAM patient placement criteria for the treatment of psychoactive substance use disorders.* Washington, DC: American Society of Addiction Medicine.

Lis, J., & Mercer, D. (1994). *Handbook for AIDS Awareness/Prevention Training.* Unpublished manuscript.

McLellan, A. T., Luborsky, L., Cacciola, J., Griffith, J., McGahan, P., & O'Brien, C. P. (1986). *Guide to the Addiction Severity Index: Background, administration, and field testing results* (DHHS Publication No. ADM 86-1419). Rockville, MD: National Institute on Drug Abuse.

Narcotics anonymous (5th ed.). (1988). Van Nuys, CA: NA World Service Office.

Prochaska, J. O., Norcross, J. C., & DiClemente, C. C. (1994). *Changing for good.* New York: William Morrow.

Project MATCH Research Group. (1997). Matching alcoholism treatments to client heterogeneity. *Journal of Studies on Alcohol, 58,* 7–29.

Robins, L. N., & Regier, D. A. (1991). *Psychiatric disorders in America: The epidemiologic catchment area study.* New York: The Free Press.

Selzer, M. L. (1971). The Michigan Alcoholism Screening Test: The quest for a new diagnostic instrument. *American Journal of Psychiatry, 127*(12), 1653–1658.

Skinner, H. A. (1982). The Drug Abuse Screening Test. *Addictive Behaviors, 7,* 363–371.

Tarter, R. E. (1990). Evaluation and treatment of adolescent substance abuse: A decision tree method. *American Journal of Drug and Alcohol Abuse, 16*(1–2), 1–46.

Tarter, R. E., & Hegedus, A. M. (1991). The Drug Use Screening Inventory: Its applications in the evaluation and treatment of alcohol and other drug abuse. *Alcohol Health and Research World, 15*(1), 65–75.

Tarter, R. E., Ott, P. J., & Mezzich, A. C. (1991). Psychometric assessment. In R. J. Frances & S. I. Miller (Eds.), *Clinical textbook of addictive disorders* (pp. 237–270). New York: The Guilford Press.

Trimpey, J. (1992). *The small book: A revolutionary alternative for overcoming alcohol and drug dependence* (Rev. ed.). New York: Dell.

For more information on Graywind Publications or TherapyWorks products, please contact The Psychological Corporation at **1–800–228–0752 (TDD 1–800–723–1318).**